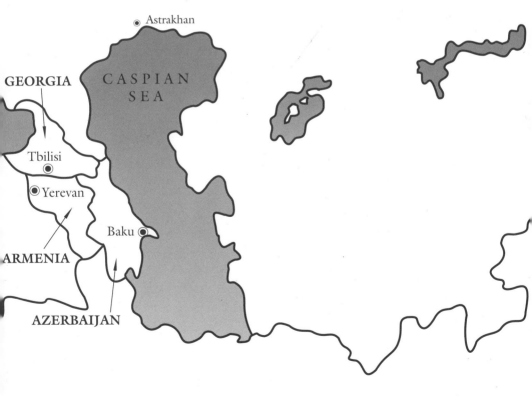

⊙ Perm

★ Yekaterinburg

⊙ Ufa

⊙ Omsk

★ Samara

⊙ Saratov

RUSSIA

⊙ Volgograd

Rostov

⊙ Karaganda

⊙ Astrakhan

GEORGIA

C A S P I A N
S E A

Tbilisi
◉

◉ Yerevan

Baku ◉

ARMENIA

AZERBAIJAN

EASTERN EUROPE AFTER COMMUNISM
★ = LDS Mission Headquarters

THE
MORNING
BREAKS

THE
MORNING
BREAKS

STORIES OF CONVERSION AND FAITH IN THE FORMER
SOVIET UNION

HOWARD L. BIDDULPH

DESERET BOOK COMPANY
SALT LAKE CITY, UTAH

Photographs throughout this book courtesy of Howard L. Biddulph.

Library of Congress Cataloging-in-Publication Data

Biddulph, Howard Lowell, 1935–

   The morning breaks : stories of conversion and faith in the former Soviet Union / by Howard Lowell Biddulph.
    p.   cm.
   Includes bibliographical references and index.
   ISBN 1-57345-152-5
   1. Mormon converts—Former Soviet republics—Biography. 2. Church of Jesus Christ of Latter-day Saints—Former Soviet republics. 3. Mormon Church—Former Soviet republics. 4. Former Soviet republics—Church history. I. Title.
BX8693.B53   1996
289.3'47—dc20   96-13912
                                      CIP

Printed in the United States of America

10 9 8 7 6 5 4 3 2 1

Awakening

In the bright Siberian sun near Ulan-Udè,
An eight-foot-thick ice sepulcher
Cracks into giant fissures
    With a mighty sonic boom,
And through the fractured crevasses
Arpeggios ripple upward from the deep,
The symphony of Lake Baikal's new birth.

Near Moscow and along the Oka,
Birches waken from the conjurer's long spell;
Gloomy grays don Lenten robes of green,
And firs shed heavy winter burdens.

Through ancient Kiev
The mighty Dnieper freely flows again;
December's frozen shroud that draped
Taras Shevchenko in the Park and Saint Volodymyr
Dissolves to water crocus beds beneath.

Along the Black Sea and the Volga,
Virgin steppes as far as eye can see
Dress up in festive blossoms—
Pinks and blues, golds and whites—
To celebrate the end of bleakness.

Alpine flowers grace the uplands
    Of the towering Caucasus,
Tenderly prevailing over avalanche and storm,
Gently occupying the hanging valleys
    Midst the stratocumulus,
Ascending to the ridge beyond the timberline.

Heroic ice sculptures,
    Reigning o'er October Revolution Square,
Wax old and melt in muddy puddles
    In the atmospheric warm front.

O while this wond'rous season lasts,
We would bear witness through the land—
From Leningrad and Tallinn, east to Magadan;
Along the Dnieper, Volga, Don, to Yerevan;
The River Ob, the Yenisei, and south to Samarkand—
Proclaim again the joyous salutation:
CHRIST IS RISEN!

                —Howard L. Biddulph
                Easter, 1990

CONTENTS

CONTENTS

ACKNOWLEDGMENTS

The idea for this book was born in a discussion that I had in Kiev, Ukraine, with Elder Mark Anderson and his wife, Sister Marilyn Anderson, of Salt Lake City. I was at that time presiding over the Ukraine Kiev Mission of The Church of Jesus Christ of Latter-day Saints, and Elder and Sister Anderson were serving as full-time missionaries in that mission (his fifth and her fourth mission for the Church). We were discussing some of the remarkable stories of spiritual conversion in the mission, and the Andersons suggested the importance of preserving and sharing these with the international Church. I want to thank them for that idea and for encouraging me to undertake this project.

It is impossible to adequately thank the many individuals who have contributed directly or otherwise to the production of this book. I would especially like to thank those new Latter-day Saints in Ukraine, Russia, and Belarus who participated in this project by sharing the stories of their spiritual conversion. A total of fifty-three gave written accounts to me, and a number of others shared their experiences in conversation with me. The total of these accounts is more than one hundred.

Their contribution is the heart and soul of this book, and their testimonies of the restored gospel of Jesus Christ have changed my life forever. I thank each of them deeply, both those few whose experiences are recounted in these pages and the many more who, for reasons of limited space, could not be specifically included.

I am particularly indebted to Olga Kuzmina and Natalya

Karabeshkina for gathering many of the written accounts of converts in Ukraine and for translating and typing much of this material. I thank Anatoly Neverov for helping me obtain conversion accounts from Belarussian Latter-day Saints.

A number of former missionaries who served in these lands also made contributions to the story. Matt Ericson, Anthony Brown, Daniel Reneau, James Harris, Lee Wilkerson, Ulrike Wein, James Karper, Quinton Spencer, and Matthew Rowe sent me written accounts of experiences. I discussed specific experiences or checked details with other former missionaries, including John Lunt, Thomas Wright, Richard Jackson, Richard Davis, Georgianna Standiford, Russell van der Werf, Aaron Love, Tania Rands, Melinda Richards, Cynthia Robbins, Bryan Jarman, Scott Suggs, Robin Curtis, Tyson Richardson, Curtis Bingham, Thomas Abbott, Rex Griffiths, Arvil Swaney, and Mary Guymon.

I benefited greatly from the wisdom and counsel of Elder Dallin H. Oaks of the Quorum of the Twelve Apostles and Elder Dennis B. Neuenschwander of the Seventy, President of the Europe East Area of The Church of Jesus Christ of Latter-day Saints.

I also found invaluable the constructive advice of Matthew K. Heiss of the Church Historical Department and the James Moyle Oral History Program of the Church. The printed compilation of his three oral history interviews with Colleen and me on September 7, 13, and 15, 1994, was a valuable resource for this project.

Susan Sheffield and Keith Terry read the entire manuscript and offered invaluable editorial and technical assistance that greatly facilitated the success of the project. Linda R. Gundry at Deseret Book was the editor for this project. Her efforts made an important contribution to the final result.

Ruth H. Biddulph, my mother, also read the entire manuscript, offering gentle and insightful critique and strong, inspiring encouragement, as always.

I must express my gratitude to our five adult children—

Barbara, Catherine, Helen, Sylvia, and Michael—and to their spouses and our thirteen grandchildren for willingly accepting a separation of three years from us. Hopefully, this manuscript will give meaning to their sacrifice.

Finally, I owe enormous gratitude to my wife, Colleen. She lived through those three years and witnessed many of the incredible experiences upon which this book is based. Her insight concerning these events has not only confirmed but also significantly deepened my own. The four volumes of her personal journals written during our mission have been an invaluable resource.

Colleen's generous consent for my use of some of her poetry, written during the mission and compiled in her book titled *Slavic Harvest* (1994), has enriched this volume. Her critique of the manuscript has been very helpful. Her support and encouragement of this project has made an important contribution to its completion.

I alone must assume full responsibility for any errors and inadequacies that remain.

This book is dedicated to that "chosen generation" whom the Lord "hath called . . . out of darkness into his marvellous light" (1 Peter 2:9).

INTRODUCTION

Before 1989, approximately one-third of the population of the earth resided in countries ruled by Communist regimes whose official ideologies proclaimed the objective of freeing human consciousness completely from the "harmful delusion" of religious belief. While this goal of universal atheism was never fully attained in any of these lands, the power of the state was utilized to greatly restrict religious liberty, and enormous resources were expended to teach atheism at every level of society through much of the twentieth century.

Then, during a remarkable two-year period (1989 to 1991), Communist rule collapsed in the Soviet Union (officially known as the Union of Soviet Socialist Republics, or USSR) and eight other countries in east-central Europe. Across this vast area from Central Europe to the Pacific, spanning twelve time zones and more than one-sixth of the land surface of the earth, approximately 425 million people reside.

Even before the fall of Communism, there was a significant beginning for freedom of conscience in the Soviet Union and east-central Europe during the latter 1980s. This was accompanied by a major religious reawakening in all of these countries, and especially among the nations and ethnic groups within the Soviet Union.

Among those who embraced new religious convictions are many converts to The Church of Jesus Christ of Latter-day Saints. Some of these have written brief accounts of their spiritual awakening and conversion. Others have orally conveyed similar accounts. The purpose of this book is to permit these

1

new Latter-day Saint voices of faith to be heard in other countries, that all might be "edified and rejoice together" (D&C 50:22; see also 84:110; Ephesians 4:12).

The coming of freedom of expression and religious liberty to the former Soviet Union and the countries of east-central Europe was a miraculous process comparable to the deliverance of ancient Israel from Egyptian bondage and Babylonian captivity in biblical times. As this momentous unshackling of the soul was occurring, many of the people of the USSR experienced a spiritual awareness in which they became active religious seekers for the first time in their lives.

Many of these religious seekers returned to the traditional churches and faiths of their lands. Others avoided denominational affiliation but became Christians in their personal convictions. Some turned to non-Christian sects and faiths. Others accepted the teachings of Protestant evangelists from the West. A rapidly growing number of new Christians have found a spiritual home in The Church of Jesus Christ of Latter-day Saints.

This is the story of the spiritual odyssey of new Latter-day Saints in some of the successor states of the former Soviet Union. Insofar as possible, this story is told from the perspective of their own testimonies and often in their own words. I have, nevertheless, attempted to integrate their diverse experiences into general themes and to provide a historical and social context.

This book combines material from fifty-three written accounts by new Latter-day Saints of their spiritual conversion, for which I have received permission to utilize. A number of others have given me oral accounts with permission to tell their experiences in this book.

In some of these accounts, I have felt it advisable not to use the real name of the individual, and in a few other cases I have been asked not to personally identify them. I have scrupulously honored each of these requests.

Except in a few cases, I have used only first names in this

*Primary children in
national costume in a
Kiev branch, 1993.*

account. Ukrainians, Russians, and Belarussians generally prefer to be addressed by fellow Latter-day Saints using their first names only, such as "Tamara," or "Sister Tamara." My use of their first names is not, therefore, an indication of disrespect, but a bowing to their wishes and normal conventions. When referring to a few top Church leaders, missionaries, and official representatives, I have used the traditional title of "president" or "sister" or "elder," followed by their family name.

These new converts are descended from many nations, peoples, and mixed ethnic groups long ruled by the Russian and Soviet empires. The dominant national origins of these new Latter-day Saints are of the Eastern Slavic peoples: Ukrainians, Russians, and Belarussians. Other nationalities also have some significant representation among these converts. Jews and Poles are significant minorities in Ukraine, Belarus, and Russia. There are also Estonians, Latvians, Lithuanians, Georgians, Armenians, Azeris, Tatars, Germans, Moldovans, Greeks, Cherkassians, and Karelo-Finns among the new Latter-day Saints. Some Russians and Ukrainians also have a mixed ancestry with the Turkic peoples of the Caucasus and

3

Central Asia. Some Eastern Slavs also intermarried with the Mongoloid peoples of East Asia.

My wife, Colleen, and I became acquainted with these new Latter-day Saints during the time I presided over the Ukraine Kiev Mission and its predecessor, the Austria Vienna East Mission of The Church of Jesus Christ of Latter-day Saints. During the years 1991 to 1994, we lived eight months in Vienna, regularly commuting into Ukraine, and twenty-nine months in Kiev.

We became acquainted with many converts from Ukraine, a number also from Belarus and Russia, and a few from Latvia, Estonia, Moldova, Armenia, and Georgia. We also came to know converts from Poland, the Czech Republic, Bulgaria, Hungary, East Germany, Albania, and some of the republics of former Yugoslavia.

Each new convert to the gospel of Jesus Christ has his or her own miraculous story to tell. Remarkably, each personal odyssey with the Spirit is unique. Every human culture across the earth also has its own distinct attributes for expressing the story of conversion.

Yet the access of all peoples to the Holy Spirit is the same. The "language of the Spirit" is understood similarly by the elect among every nation, kindred, tongue, and people of the earth. The process of the "mighty change of heart" toward the Lord is the same, and his spiritual blessings to all people who will receive him are the same, as Ammon and his brethren learned during their ministry to the Lamanites: "Now my brethren, we see that God is mindful of every people, whatsoever land they may be in; yea, he numbereth his people, and his bowels of mercy are over all the earth" (Alma 26:37).

In telling the stories of these Latter-day Saints, I have occasionally quoted short passages from other works. Parenthetical citations following these quotations give only the author, title, and page number of the quoted material. Full publication information for each source is found in the bibliography following the final chapter of this book.

The spiritual awakening of the soul from the Communist version of "scientific atheism" is a beautiful and inspiring story. There is space in one book to present only a few of the many accounts that have been offered to me. I do so with the hope that these new voices of faith will edify the Saints in other lands and that they will help build a bridge of love and understanding among peoples of faith across the earth.

Chapter 1

"PREPARE YE FOR THAT WHICH IS TO COME"

*"Prepare ye, prepare ye for that which is to
come, for the Lord is nigh."*

—Doctrine and Covenants 1:12

It happened on a beautiful Sunday at the beginning of August 1961 in Moscow's Central Baptist Church. I was sitting on the front row of a side balcony that permitted me to look down at the faces of parishioners who filled the pews and jammed the aisles on the ground floor of the church.

That year I was completing a summer program in the Soviet Union for my graduate studies at Indiana University. My conversations on religion with several new acquaintances in Moscow and Leningrad had kindled a strong desire within me to share my faith in Jesus Christ. Yet I was painfully aware of the restrictions against religious expression in that land. Nikita Khrushchev's renewed campaign of state persecution of religious organizations and believers was at its peak in 1961.

Westerners visiting churches in the USSR were often moved by the deep piety of the people, and I was no exception. I remembered hearing earlier of the visit of Elder Ezra Taft Benson of the Quorum of the Twelve Apostles to this very building two years before, when he was serving as secretary of agriculture under United States president Dwight D. Eisenhower. Elder Benson had been deeply moved here, and the public witness of Christ he had shared in this building had touched many who were present, according to the Reverend Ilya Orlov, with whom I had visited before the service.

I looked down upon a sea of deeply devout, yearning faces. Tears were streaming down the cheeks of many. I sensed in these people an incredible spiritual desire for light and truth. My own emotions overflowed, and inwardly I asked, *When, O Father, shall they enjoy the opportunity to receive the fulness of thy restored gospel?* Immediately I felt a peaceful, warm, comforting feeling that seemed to respond, *In mine own due time they shall receive.*

The Day of the Berlin Wall

A few days later our study group flew to Stalingrad (now known as Volgograd). After visiting this historic city, we took a riverboat down the southern part of the Volga, across the Volga-Don Canal, and along the Don River to the city of Rostov.

It was a very interesting journey past thatch-roofed villages. I felt as if I had passed through a time warp and was back in the nineteenth century. Because of a painful sunburn, I stayed in the shade of a lower deck during much of the cruise, but on the last day I felt well enough to go on the top deck to view the small settlement we were then approaching, a few kilometers upstream from metropolitan Rostov.

I studied for a moment the little streets of this dingy town that rose steeply up the hill from the docks. Then, suddenly, I could see future missionaries of The Church of Jesus Christ of Latter-day Saints on those very streets. I could see that there would someday be members of the LDS Church in that village and that organized branches would exist within the vicinity.

My first reaction to this impression was to question it. Future missionary work and Latter-day Saints in Moscow were believable to my thinking, but this remote outpost of the eighteenth-century Don Cossacks seemed hard to visualize as a gathering place for a future Zion.

Yet again I received the same impression, this time more powerful than the first: *Latter-day Saint missionaries will one day walk these very streets; members of the Church will be here; organized branches will be in the vicinity.* After that I no longer doubted that this impression was of the Lord.

I quickly climbed the stairway from the deck to the bridge and asked the captain for the name of this little town, so that I could record the experience in my journal. He told me it was called Aksai. I logged that name in my journal, along with a brief account of my experience. Whether or not its fulfillment would come in my lifetime remained to be seen, but I felt confident that one day the gospel would be taught in the Soviet Union, including this region, and it was important for me to record in my journal this premonition of that future event.

Afterward, this experience remained silently stored in my journal for many years, known only to members of my immediate family and one or two others. The date I recorded for it was 13 August 1961. A week later I learned of the erection of the Berlin Wall by the Soviet Union. I realized much later, however, that my experience at Aksai had come on the very day of the erection of the wall. How strange it now seems to me to have received such a premonition on the very day that the Soviet Union erected that great barrier against freedom, for the fulfillment of my impression would be possible only after the fall of that infamous wall. Because of my involvement in those then-future events, I must tell how I became interested in the Soviet Union.

Preparation

My interest in the Soviet Union began at age seven as I studied a volume owned by my parents on world geography. For some reason I was particularly drawn to the pages showing the geography of the Union of Soviet Socialist Republics. Russia was represented in red, Ukraine in yellow, and the remaining republics in a variety of other colors. Over and over

I tried to pronounce the names of cities, territories, and rivers. I also located the USSR on my world globe, telling myself that someday I would visit that land.

Certain passages in my patriarchal blessing, which I received at age thirteen, hinted at things that caused me to hope that one day I might preach the gospel in that land. The patriarchal blessing of my younger sister Susan explicitly foretold that at least one of her children would preach the gospel in "the land of Russia." (Her daughter, Sherry Sheffield, would serve in the Russia St. Petersburg Mission from 1992 to 1994.) Later I learned that my future wife, Colleen, had received a similar promise in her patriarchal blessing, that through the services of her future family, the gospel would be preached "in the land of Russia."

These expectations and desires guided my career choice and my university studies at both undergraduate and advanced postgraduate levels. Then, for almost thirty years, I was a political science professor, specializing in the Soviet Union, at Rutgers University in New Jersey and the University of Victoria in Canada. At Victoria I was chair of the Department of Political Science.

Four times during those three decades my professional writing on the Soviet Union involved me in research projects in various cities of the USSR. I spent time in Moscow, Leningrad, Kiev, Tbilisi, and Yerevan. On each trip I sensed that one day the gospel would be preached in each of those cities. I never got over that impression.

One day as I was reading in *History of the Church*, I was both intrigued and reassured by the Prophet Joseph Smith's remarkable statement in 1843 about how the bringing of the gospel "to the people of that vast empire" of Russia is a subject "to which is attached some of the most important things concerning the advancement and building up of the kingdom of God in the last days, which cannot be explained at this time" (Joseph Smith, *History of the Church*, 6:41).

In April 1974, President Spencer W. Kimball opened to

Primary children in Simferopol Branch. Spring 1994.

the leaders and members of the Church a visionary plan for taking the gospel to all the earth, challenging Latter-day Saints to make the quiet resolve to "lengthen our stride." The Saints were asked to pray that barriers to the spreading of the gospel, such as the Iron Curtain, might be removed. He promised that the Lord would "open the doors" in those lands denied the gospel—as soon as members of the Church were prepared in faith to walk through them. During this time a number of Church leaders prophesied specifically that the Lord would miraculously open a way for the Soviet Union to receive the gospel when members of the Church were ready.

I became aware of the beginnings of missionary work in Moscow and Leningrad while on a trip there in the spring of 1990. The USSR was in the midst of Mikhail Gorbachev's attempted political reforms, and greater freedom of religion had already commenced. I was briefly visiting Moscow to arrange for a more extensive sabbatical research year at the Institute of State and Law during 1991 and 1992. After making all necessary arrangements for my sabbatical residency at the Institute, I was invited by an American acquaintance working in Moscow to attend a Book of Mormon study group he was having at his apartment with ten Russians and an Estonian. It was an inspiring evening to meet people whose reading of the Book of Mormon had already converted them to the gospel.

The following Sunday on my flight home, I stopped in Leningrad to attend worship services in the first branch of local members. I met missionaries from the Finland Helsinki Mission who had been sent there by their mission president, Steven R. Mecham. I was thrilled to meet the Russian branch president, Yuri Terebinin, and other local leaders who conducted the meetings of the branch.

President Terebinin invited me to speak in sacrament service. I cannot describe how wonderful it was to openly bear testimony of the gospel to Russians in their own language. I was overcome with emotion at the sight of the gospel making its way into the Soviet Union, saying over and over to myself: *I have waited so long to witness this! I can hardly believe the time has finally arrived!*

I returned home so excited that it was difficult to concentrate on my work at the university. I explained to Colleen what I had seen and my great desire for us to go on a mission together to the Soviet Union. My enthusiasm must have infected her; she was eager to go with me.

The Call

The problem with my leaving the university and Colleen her elementary school teaching job was simply that we would not reach retirement age (sixty-five) until the year 2000. That was a decade away, and I expressed fears that by that time the liberal reform era of Gorbachev might come to an end, and events would then snuff out further opportunity to preach the gospel in the USSR. I explored the possibility of taking a nonprofessional leave of absence or, if necessary, an early retirement, but found that neither option was open to me. Still we looked forward to sharing the gospel in Moscow during our sabbatical year of research.

A few months later, on 22 January 1991, Elder L. Tom Perry of the Quorum of the Twelve Apostles interviewed

Colleen and me in Victoria. Four days later, on 26 January, President Thomas S. Monson telephoned us and extended a call to me as mission president over an unspecified Russian-speaking mission, effective 1 July 1991. We accepted this call with inexpressible joy, even though we expected that it would be necessary to resign our teaching positions.

The next morning, however, I arrived at my university office to find a personal letter from the president of the university, offering an unusual one-time opportunity to take retirement ten years early at a favorable settlement. This special opportunity was offered only to those scheduled for retirement in the year 2000.

I sat in my office and stared with wonder at the letter. I had told no one at the university of our mission call. Now suddenly the very thing that had concerned us most about the future had been carefully orchestrated by the Lord to allow us to move ahead with our mission. We poured out our hearts in thanksgiving to the Lord for this miraculous blessing. Additional miracles helped us sell our home immediately and arrange all of our personal effects so we could leave for our mission.

Colleen also was able to arrange a favorable early retirement from her teaching position. She had always believed that the promise in her patriarchal blessing about preaching the gospel in "the land of Russia" referred to her descendants, not to her. But one year before the call came, she felt inspired to begin her study of the Russian language. She completed a one-year introductory course at the university before leaving for the mission, which gave her a head start on learning Russian.

The day before we left for the Missionary Training Center in Provo, Utah, we were informed that our assignment would be to preside over missionaries serving in Kiev, Ukraine. We would live initially in Vienna, Austria, but it was the hope of the Brethren that three new missions in the Soviet Union would soon officially be announced: one in Moscow, one in

President Howard and Sister Colleen Biddulph in Kiev.

St. Petersburg (formerly Leningrad), and one in Kiev. We would then move into the country and preside over one of those three missions.

Prophecies Fulfilled

In July 1990, Latter-day Saint missionaries arrived in Moscow under the direction of President Gary L. Browning of the Finland Helsinki East Mission. Converts were baptized who initially attended an international branch in Moscow. In March 1991, the first branch totally administered by local Russians opened in Moscow—almost thirty years after the spiritual premonition I received at the Central Baptist Church.

The subsequent impressions that came to me during my visit thirty years before to Aksai, near Rostov-on-the-Don, began to be fulfilled in the fall of 1991. As mission president, I was assigned by Elder Hans B. Ringger of the Seventy, president of the Europe Area, to visit specified cities in Ukraine, southern Russia, and Moldova to determine their potential for future missionary work. One of these assigned cities was Rostov-on-the-Don.

Elder Ivan Stratov (middle) opened LDS missionary work in Ukraine.

On 27 November 1991, Elder Ivan Stratov (a Russian-Australian from Melbourne) and I were the first missionaries to visit Rostov-on-the-Don and the nearby suburban community of Aksai. At Aksai we walked up those very streets I had seen thirty years before from a boat on the Don River. We mingled with the people and met some choice contacts.

Just three years later, in 1994, the first assigned missionaries began proselyting in Rostov from the Russia Samara Mission. On 1 July 1994, the Russia Rostov Mission officially commenced. Soon there were a number of converts to the Church in the Rostov area, and several branches were quickly organized.

The premonition I received on the day the Berlin Wall was erected was completely fulfilled five years after the wall's great collapse in 1989. The Soviet Union and its East European empire were no more. By the mid-1990s, missionaries were serving in fifteen new missions from Central Europe to central Siberia, nine of which were in the former Soviet Union. Converts to the LDS Church already resided in approximately thirty cities of the former USSR.

All this was unthinkable to me in 1961. But the Lord,

almost imperceptibly, had been preparing the land and the people, as well as the missionaries, for the coming harvest of the restored gospel of Jesus Christ. Colleen wrote the following poem to express her joy at the reopening of these lands to missionary work.

The Harvest

So vast is the field,
The laborers few.
We serve the true Master,
And His will we do.
The famine is ended,
The long drought is gone.
The seed has been planted;
We greet a new dawn.

So long we have waited
To work this parched field.
To water its furrows
And dream of great yield.
The field is now white,
The harvest is choice.
We thrust in our sickles;
We reap and rejoice!

—Colleen C. Biddulph

Chapter 2

"SEARCHING IN DARKNESS"

"Searching in darkness, nations have wept;
Watching for dawn, their vigil they've kept."
—*Hymns*, no. 264

An old Russian and Ukrainian religious legend predicted the coming of the anti-Christ to their lands. Many Ukrainians, Russians, and Belarussians who have read the Book of Mormon comment on the close similarity of the Communist doctrine of scientific atheism to the teachings of Korihor, the ancient Nephite anti-Christ (see Alma 30:12–28).

I agree with this observation. Many aspects of the Leninist critique of religion, and especially of Christ, correspond closely to the arguments of Korihor. The Leninist version of Marxism, which enjoyed a protected monopoly over ideas in the Soviet Union for more than seventy years, was the most pervasive anti-Christ doctrine of the twentieth century. Yet the light of Christ continued to shine in darkness, although the darkness comprehended it not. This light attracted many souls (see John 1:5, 9).

Resisting the "Science of Atheism"

Natasha grew up near the Ukrainian city of Kherson, where the Dnieper River empties into the Black Sea. She was a brilliant student and was one of the few in her area chosen to go to Moscow with a full fellowship to complete her graduate studies at Moscow State Pedagogical University, a top institution for training professors to teach the techniques of the Russian language.

In Moscow she obtained her candidate of sciences degree (comparable to a Ph.D. in the West). All of her marks were "excellent," except in the required course of "scientific atheism," in which she received a "poor" mark. For such a bright young student, why the poor marks in a class that should not have been difficult for her? It was her attitude, not her academic skill.

In the USSR, all educational institutions from kindergarten to advanced universities had required course material, supervised by the Communist Party, designed to teach that all religion is "harmful superstition" and that atheism is the only socially acceptable and "scientific" outlook. The Soviet Constitution formally granted citizens "the right to conduct religious worship or atheistic propaganda" (Article 52), but not "religious propaganda." Religion could be taught legally only within a government-registered church or "house of prayer" to people at least eighteen years of age. Many Catholic and Baptist leaders were arrested for trying to teach children, but the Orthodox Church strictly complied with the law.

Natasha had argued with her scientific atheism instructor. She disagreed with him about the validity of his evidence for the assertion that God does not exist. The professor quoted her the statement by Yury Gagarin, a Soviet cosmonaut who had been in space and "found no God out there." He simply quoted the dogmas of the party about religion. By this time, Natasha had read the philosophical debates about the existence of God in the works of Russian writers like Dostoyevsky and Tolstoy. Compared to their analyses, she found the dogmas her professor spouted to be totally inadequate.

Natasha's other professors urged her to retake the final examination for the atheism course and to answer the questions in the way the professor expected, so that her "poor" mark would not appear on an otherwise brilliant academic record. Natasha had integrity and refused to do this. She stood on principle, no matter how it might affect her academic record. She had agonized long over the question, Does God exist? In all her readings in literature and philosophy, she was confused as to her own personal view and beliefs. She simply refused to accept uncritically the Communistic dogmas on the nonexistence of God.

Valery's Background

But Natasha was not alone. Her husband, Valery, was also a brilliant student. He had grown up in a small town, not far from the city of Zaporozhe in Ukraine, and was the son of dedicated Communists who had held positions of local leadership in the party. He had been taught nothing concerning religion by his parents, but his grandmother was a believer.

Valery's grandmother decided when he was a child to have him baptized into the Russian Orthodox Church, but his parents, who learned of her plans, removed him from her at the last moment to avoid this religious sacrament. It was not uncommon for children of members of the Communist Party to be secretly baptized by a grandmother or a parent; but it was a serious offense and a black mark against the family if the Party found out, since its members were expected to be "exemplary atheists." In this case, however, Valery's parents were opposed, as a matter of principle, to religious baptism.

His excellent grades in school won Valery admission to Moscow State University, plus a stipend. It was a prestigious opportunity in the USSR, especially for a student from a distant, small town in Ukraine. Party and other connections were decisive in obtaining such opportunities in the USSR. On the other hand, as a matter of party policy, youth who were known to be religious or to come from the families of religious believers were systematically excluded from higher educational opportunities. Although there were believers in God in higher education and among the "creative and scientific intelligentsia," for the most part they were secret believers, what one scholar called "Nicodemuses."

On the heels of his brilliant scholarship at Moscow State University, Valery was admitted to the Institute of International Relations of the USSR Council of Ministers. This was an elite training center for future career diplomats in the Soviet government.

He had studied English for many years, but it was at the institute that Valery obtained an excellent command of the language. The institute stocked American books, magazines, and periodicals that were not available to the Soviet public, and Valery read them avidly. For some reason he could not understand, Valery felt especially drawn to read about Utah. This was an intellectual curiosity only; he was not at that time a seeker of religion.

Valery was assigned by his superiors, however, to be not an American affairs specialist but a Southeast Asian economic specialist. He was shipped off to Hanoi, Vietnam, to learn the languages, culture, and political economy of that region as part of his graduate education.

Valery was back in Moscow during the Gorbachev era. He noted the increasing freedom of inquiry and expression. He was fascinated to see that most professors and scholars seemed relieved that they no longer had to defend scientific atheism. It was evident that many of the Communist Party's large cadre of scholars and instructors lacked enthusiasm for teaching atheism or other ideological dogmas they were assigned to defend. Among the intelligentsia, many secret religious believers "came out of the closet," openly discussing their faith.

The economic crisis that accompanied the decline of Communist control and increasing freedom of expression led many educated people, as well as ordinary citizens, to feel a sense of spiritual vacuum or confusion in their lives. Many who later became LDS converts described going through this experience.

Natasha and Valery were among those who experienced these feelings. They and many others were considering not only questions about their political and economic future but also deeper, more profound questions of human existence: Who am I? What is the meaning of life, and what is our personal destiny after death? Where can we find a valid standard of moral conduct? Where is truth, justice, beauty, purity, love, and hope for man?

To answer these questions, members of the intelligentsia and also ordinary citizens began to turn their attention to the study of religion. The question was, however, where to turn to find the answers to these religious questions. Should one return to the traditional church? Should one explore foreign or new religious confessions? What about reading the Bible or other religious works on one's own without denominational affiliation? The result of all these vital questions was a remarkable upsurge of interest in religion as the influence of the Communist view of the world began to crumble, especially during the last years of the Gorbachev era.

Searching for a Spiritual Home

Vyacheslav (Slava) and Zoya, husband and wife, were among those searching for spiritual answers. Both are of Jewish ancestry, so their families had suffered the tragedy of anti-Semitism for generations in Ukraine and throughout the Russian empire.

One of Zoya's great-grandfathers was murdered in the presence of his wife and children during a pogrom in the latter nineteenth century. Before Zoya's birth, her mother and grandparents had survived World War II by fleeing eastward to Kazakhstan, just ahead of the German occupation troops who shot Jews systematically, massacring two hundred thousand Jews and others in a ravine in Kiev called Babi Yar. Zoya's father served in the Soviet Red Army.

Slava's grandfather Gulko, a poor young man with a bride in tow, arrived in Kiev just before World War I. At the end of the war, he narrowly escaped death when he was seized by the anti-Semitic troops of Simon Petliura's Ukrainian Nationalist Army during the civil war after the Bolshevik Revolution. He

Kiev District President Vyacheslav (Slava) Gulko and his wife, Zoya, at the Freiberg Germany Temple in June 1993.

managed to flee his captors in the dead of a cold winter night, traveling without outer clothing, a coat, or boots. He survived and returned to hide with his wife and family. Gulko became a very devout Jewish participant in the Kiev synagogue, promising God that he would give his only son to be a rabbi to an increasingly atheistic society.

The son was Slava's father, who dashed these fervent hopes by becoming an atheist like most of his generation. Then Josef Stalin forcibly closed the Kiev synagogue. Slava's father became a young officer in World War II and was seriously wounded during the conflict. His wounds were thought fatal, but miraculously he recovered and returned home.

Although Slava's father was an atheist, Grandfather Gulko insisted on having his grandson Slava circumcised a few days after his birth in 1950. In his early youth Slava was greatly embarrassed to be the only one of his Jewish and Gentile companions who had undergone this rite of Judaism, but he later regarded it as a singular honor, showing that he was set apart for a special relationship with God.

Unfortunately, Slava's grandfather died when Slava was nine years old. This ended the family's religious influence in his early life. His father raised him an atheist. Even so, he later studied the ancient history of his people. He read a book detailing the history of the destruction of the temple in Jerusalem and the fall of that city to Rome. Still in his youth, he developed a strong inner feeling that he was descended from the great King David.

As gifted students, Slava and Zoya, like their peers, were taught an atheistic perspective in school. By the ninth grade, Slava had chosen a career as a nuclear physicist and later fulfilled his dream with great distinction, becoming a department head in an elite government research faculty on nuclear physics. Zoya, who was gifted in languages (especially English), became an instructor of English in a special school in Kiev that was attended by children of the Ukrainian politically elite. Her skills included translating.

Slava had come to accept the notion that "religion is the opium of the people," but by 1989 he and Zoya began to feel the same spiritual emptiness that enveloped the minds of others. Aware of the void in their lives, they made a conscious decision to begin a search for spirituality. First they tried a return to Judaism. They read the Torah carefully and attended synagogue. This failed to fulfill their spiritual longings and desires. They continued to feel lonely and spiritually bereft but still hopeful of ultimate success in their quest for spiritual growth.

Next they encountered the Baha'i faith. At first they found its ecumenical objective of uniting all faiths in one to be appealing. Soon, however, they became dissatisfied and discontinued their association with the movement. After this stint in religious discovery, Slava and Zoya began to investigate Christianity, reading the New Testament and coming close to an acceptance of Jesus as the Messiah.

In exploring various Christian beliefs, they could not bring themselves to seriously investigate Russian Orthodoxy. Instead, Slava and Zoya investigated Protestantism through "The Campus Crusade for Christ" program shortly after its arrival in Kiev. That failed to satisfy their spiritual quest, so they moved in the direction of Roman Catholicism during a long visit to Poland. Skepticism and spiritual unfulfillment persisted, but as late as the fall of 1991, they had not given up their search. Slava and Zoya were yet to find a spiritual home in Christ and to be major participants in establishing his kingdom in Ukraine.

Seeking for Answers

There were others searching for spiritual fulfillment. One of these was Leonid. He was the son of the assistant to the president of the Ukrainian Academy of Sciences, and his mother was also a member of the academy. As Leonid tells it: "I grew up absorbing a materialist understanding of the world. I was an atheist. At least I had been taught to be, like so many others."

As part of an effort to improve his life and health, Leonid began to study Eastern philosophy and medicine. This led him to study Eastern religions, such as Hinduism, Islam, Buddhism, Taoism, and Yoga. Leonid felt a longing for something he could not fully grasp or articulate. He describes the feeling as "an expectation of something beautiful that would happen in my life." This impelled him to continue his search.

Sergei had also been raised as an atheist. Like most citizens in the Soviet Union, he had no access to the Bible or other religious materials. As he moved into higher education, however, Sergei had access to a copy of the New Testament at his institute, though he read it only out of intellectual curiosity. He was not yet ready to seek God; in fact, to commit to such a course would have jeopardized his educational opportunities.

"Five years later," he recalled, "I met a Christian believer, and I argued a lot with him about the Bible. I asked questions that no one could answer: Why, if God really spoke through prophets anciently, are there no prophets now? If there are really miracles in the Bible, why are there no such miracles and revelations now? Has God's attitude changed toward us?" Repeatedly he asked these questions when confronted by Christian believers, and no one could answer them adequately. Sergei waited decades for the true answers to his questions.

Dmitry the Believer

Dmitry is a Russian, born in Siberia. He became a Christian while serving in the Soviet Red Army, at which time he read and accepted the New Testament. After completing military service, he enrolled in one of the major Russian Orthodox seminaries in the USSR, completing the program with high marks. Dmitry was deeply converted to Christ but was unable to accept many of the doctrines and practices of the Russian Church. For this reason he purposefully resisted ordination to the office of priest, though he continued as an activist in directing choirs and organizing Sunday school classes.

Dmitry's religious activism got him into serious trouble with authorities. Arrested and convicted of illegal religious activity, he was sentenced to serve three years in brutal forced-labor camps that Solzhenitsyn and Moroz vividly described in their writings.

During the Brezhnev era, a few churches and prayer houses of the Russian Orthodox and Evangelical Christian Baptist faiths were legally registered and permitted to function with ordained clergy. There were also many unregistered "underground" (and therefore illegal) religious bodies functioning, but those who participated in such groups were subject to arrest. Even legally invested priests could get into serious trouble if they were considered "activists" for the faith. Priests were expected to perform the sacraments of the church for those attending services, but not to get involved in actively propagating their Christian faith.

Prior to his prison sentence, Dmitry was an activist who was unordained and operating classes that were not apparently registered. Upon his release, Dmitry was permitted to live in a large city in Ukraine, where he associated with the university. He was granted the opportunity to teach a course at the university during the more liberal period of Gorbachev's rule. He titled his course "The Bible As Literature." Even then such a

24

Some of the early missionaries who worked in Donetsk, Kharkov, Gorlovka, Dnepropetrovsk, and Makayevka.

course was controversial. His classes were, in fact, a rigorous study of biblical theology and Russian religious philosophy. As a brilliant teacher, he gathered a considerable following who were attracted to his course. This brought Dmitry to the attention of the Russian Orthodox bishop, who, in the absence of an adequate seminary, invited all new acolyte priests to take Dmitry's course. Protestant pastors also enrolled. His fame as a religious teacher spread throughout the region.

Dmitry was a devoted believer in the Bible, yet within himself he was not satisfied with any religious system or interpretation of the holy scriptures he had studied, whether Orthodox, Catholic, or Protestant. Through those trying years he remained a hungry Christian seeker after religious truth, while purchasing and reading every new and old book on religion that appeared on the shelves.

The single room where Dmitry lived was part of an old, collapsing, prerevolutionary building filled from floor to ceiling with religious books, journals, and magazines. He kept open a narrow corridor among these stacks of books and journals that was wide enough for passage and a bed. His restless religious search consumed his life.

Because of his diligence, one day in the future Dmitry

25

would find a book of scripture that would totally alter his life. He would discover the Book of Mormon.

Lifetime Seeker of Mormonism

Pyotr is a Belarussian physician in his forties who lives in Minsk. He attended the Baptist Church, but throughout his life has called himself a "Mormon." His father, now deceased, became acquainted during World War II with a Latter-day Saint serviceman in France who taught and baptized him.

Pyotr's father returned from the war with a small notebook containing some translations of passages from the Book of Mormon. He dared not bring any printed religious materials home at that time, because it was illegal and very dangerous to do so. From that small notebook, Pyotr declares, his father raised him to be a Mormon. Pyotr loved the passages of scripture and read them over and over. He also understood and strictly observed the Word of Wisdom, abstaining from alcohol, tobacco, tea, and coffee throughout his life.

Pyotr called himself a Mormon not only to his associates at the Baptist Church but also to many of his other friends. He claims he even told this to the military draft board. Pyotr dreamed of the time when he might actually read the Book of Mormon in its entirety and be baptized officially into The Church of Jesus Christ of Latter-day Saints.

All these future Latter-day Saints were seeking in the dark. Still, the Spirit of the Lord was preparing them to accept the restored gospel of Jesus Christ when it would come to the Soviet Union. They awaited spiritual deliverance and were ready to receive that "marvellous work and a wonder" (Isaiah 29:14) that was yet to come.

Chapter 3

"HE . . . BRAKE THEIR BANDS IN SUNDER"

"He brought them out of darkness and the shadow of death, and brake their bands in sunder."

—Psalm 107:14

Nineteen eighty-five was a fateful year in the Soviet Union. Mikhail Sergeyevich Gorbachev, the youngest member of the Soviet leadership, was chosen by his colleagues in the Politburo to be general secretary of the Communist Party of the Soviet Union. It came at a time of unprecedented deterioration of economic performance in the USSR. The party leadership recognized that economic crisis would jeopardize both the domestic stability of the country and its international power.

After making some modest attempts to improve economic performance, Gorbachev and his supporters formulated a major plan for economic reform, which they called "restructuring" (or in Russian, *perestroika*). This new reform had important implications for the freedoms that were yet to come. Initially, perestroika involved only economic measures: the decentralizing of economic decision making, the replacing of "command from above" with contracts between individual enterprises, and material incentives to encourage greater worker productivity.

Gorbachev and his associates soon came to recognize, however, that economic stagnation could not be resolved by

27

simply decentralizing the economy and devising new incentives. Poor economic performance, he believed, was rooted in worker apathy caused by a feeling of powerlessness. Workers and citizens felt they had no control over their own lives. Gorbachev was sensitive to the times and felt that the causes of the growing economic crisis were political, social, and spiritual in nature and that something had to be done.

In August 1986, the newspaper *Pravda* carried a statement from Gorbachev declaring that perestroika required a "genuine revolution in the minds and hearts of people." The working people must shed mental and spiritual authoritarianism in order to overcome "alienation from their work." People must be free to openly express differing opinions and to participate in making decisions. This was a startling declaration in light of the entrenched, conservative Communists that ran all levels of the government.

Everyone, he came to believe, should be free to criticize higher officials as well as fellow workers publicly, even in the media. This he called "openness" (or *glasnost*). Glasnost became public policy throughout the country in 1986 and 1987. Those who watched affairs in the USSR began to feel that glasnost might be the beginning of freedom of expression. Soon Gorbachev began to speak of the importance of a "pluralism of opinions" in all public discourse. He felt that such expression was healthy for the people and that it would empower them.

Then, in 1988, Gorbachev concluded through experience that glasnost could be effective only if there existed legal safeguards for freedom of expression against retaliation by officials, who would stand firmly in the way if there were no teeth in glasnost. He felt that freedom of speech and of the press must be protected by law.

Freedom of expression, however, in itself was not enough. The entire government needed to be democratized by allowing citizens to independently participate in politics. This had to include the right to seek office in competitive elections and the right to organize autonomous groups to support legislative proposals. The party and the state should relinquish control so that social groups could become self-managing and a genuine "civil society" could develop. All of this Gorbachev called "democratization."

Stephen White, a British analyst of Soviet politics, summarizes the momentous political changes that then occurred:

> Competitive elections were held for the first working parliament in Soviet history. The media began to reflect a variety of points of view. The economy was exposed to private and cooperative ownership as part of a wider transition to market relations. An attempt was made to construct a "renewed federation" that would take the place of the over-centralized union of the previous seventy years. And "new thinking" in international affairs led to a series of changes in East-West relations. (Stephen White, *After Gorbachev*, p. ix)

Gorbachev did not at first go so far, however, as to propose that rival parties be permitted to compete with the Communist Party. After all, the General Secretary saw himself as a Communist as well as a reformer. It was the party that put him in power. He hoped that a reformed party could voluntarily win the support of the people and allow greater political and social autonomy. He was frank enough to admit and declare that if, however, the Communist Party could not maintain the voluntary support of the people, it no longer deserved the right to rule. Gorbachev boldly stated this in 1988.

Religious Reform Begins

Throughout the upheaval of the era, Gorbachev counted on his liberal reforms to win the support of intellectuals and the masses against the hard-line authoritarians in the Communist Party apparatus who were blocking his policies. Instead, glasnost and democratization unleashed new political forces that the party could no longer control, and the failure of economic reform led to greater mass disillusionment with Gorbachev and the party.

Freedom of thought and social organization would not be complete, Gorbachev realized, without including religion. While there is no evidence that he was personally religious, from 1986 onward he had experts drafting legislation for freedom of religion.

This was a difficult and contentious battle between "new thinking" reformers and hard-liners determined to be true to the behest of Lenin, who had declared: "Every religious idea, every idea of God, even flirting with the idea of God, is unutterable vileness, vileness of the most dangerous kind, 'contagion' of the most abominable kind. Millions of sins, filthy deeds, acts of violence, and physical 'contagions' . . . are far less dangerous than the subtle, spiritual idea of a God" (V. I. Lenin, *Selected Works*, 11:675–76).

On 29 April 1988, Mikhail Gorbachev received Patriarch Pimen of the Russian Orthodox Church and other synod members for a formal meeting in the Kremlin. This was the first formal meeting between party and church leaders since 4 September 1943, when Stalin sought and received church support to mobilize citizens for the war with German fascism.

Undoubtedly, one motivation for this second historic accommodation between party and church leaders was to again mobilize popular support, this time against the powerful institutional foes of perestroika.

The Soviet government gave material support and publicity to the grand celebration of the millennium of Orthodox Christianity in Kiev and Moscow. This took place from 5 June through 16 June 1988. Many foreign dignitaries were invited, with the electronic and print media of the USSR covering the event. The celebration offered high visibility. All these events signaled the rehabilitation of the Russian Orthodox Church as a social institution and as a worthy part of national Russian, Ukrainian, and Belarussian culture.

Growing Religious Ferment

Meanwhile, during the period of the latter 1980s, government bodies had quietly been permitting the registration of local churches. During this period it was still very difficult for faiths other than the Russian Orthodox Church to receive legal registration. This was especially true in Ukraine, where the Greek Catholic Church and autocephalic churches had been major underground faiths since the Stalin era.

In fact, the chairman of the Ukrainian State Council for Religious Affairs claimed erroneously in 1989 that "in hundreds of statements, signed by tens of thousands of citizens, there is a request to register only Orthodox Church societies and not that of other religions" (Keston News Service, 16 March 1989, pp. 8–9).

Although denied legal registration by the Ukrainian government, the Autocephalic (independent Ukrainian) Orthodox Church, suppressed by Stalin in 1930, began to openly participate again. In August 1989, the Lvov Parish of the Church of Saints Peter and Paul threw off jurisdiction of the Russian Moscow Patriarchate and announced its adherence to the Ukrainian Autocephalic Orthodox Church.

A number of other Orthodox churches in the western part of Ukraine followed suit. In October 1990, the Autocephalic Church was finally officially registered.

The Greek Catholic Church follows the liturgy of Eastern Christianity but subordinates itself to the Pope in Rome. This church was suppressed in the Stalin era, and its buildings and parishioners were handed over to the Russian Orthodox Church. Like the Autocephalic Church, it remained an operating underground church for fifty years—a monumental struggle for those who kept the religious flame burning.

In 1989 Greek Catholics began to openly participate in services in many cities of western Ukraine, although they had not been granted official recognition. On 18 June 1989, one hundred thousand people seeking freedom of religious expression gathered openly in Ivano-Frankivsk. On 29 October 1989, Ukrainian Catholics seized the Church of the Transfiguration in Lvov, which had originally been theirs. More than fifty churches in western Ukraine followed suit by transferring their affiliation from the Russian Orthodox Patriarchate in Moscow to the Vatican in Rome.

It was learned that Gorbachev was going to Rome for an accommodation with Pope John Paul II on 1 December 1989. The announcement sent tens of thousands of Ukrainian Catholics into the streets in Lvov on 26 November, just a week before Gorbachev left for Rome. They demonstrated for their rights to be legally recognized in Ukraine. After Gorbachev visited the Vatican, Myroslav Cardinal Lubachivsky, primate of the Ukrainian Church, was permitted to return after fifty-three years in exile.

Events on the religious front were beginning to move rapidly toward freedom of worship. Early in 1990 the Ukrainian government permitted the registration of six hundred Catholic parishes in western Ukraine. Already in Lithuania the Vilnius Cathedral had been returned to the dominant Roman Catholic Church. The government permitted registration of new parishes by this time.

Among Protestants there was a growing avalanche of involvement in religious affairs. The Baptists, Adventists, and some other Russian Protestant sects that had existed in the Russian Empire before 1917 were on the move. A few of these had remained legally registered throughout the Soviet era, but the Reform Baptists, Pentacostals, and Jehovah's Witnesses functioned illegally.

In Russia new congregations of Baptists, Adventists, Pentacostals, Lutherans, Methodists, and Jehovah's Witnesses received legal recognition in 1988 and 1989, but in Ukraine these groups had trouble obtaining registration until 1990. The Church of Jesus Christ of Latter-day Saints was registered by the government of the Russian Republic in 1991. This was a major achievement for the Church. The Baha'i World Faith and the Unification Church were also granted official registration that same year.

The New Law on Religious Freedom

In May 1990, after four years of discussion, sharp debate, and delay, the draft of the new "Law on the Freedom of Conscience and Religious Organizations" was read in the USSR Supreme Soviet (Parliament). This historic law was finally enacted on 26 September 1990 in Moscow, going into effect on October 9.

The new law was a major thrust forward for freedom of religion; it guaranteed full legal status for religious organizations, freedom of conscience, and freedom of worship. The separation of church and state was proclaimed, as well as the equality of all faiths. Religious groups were ensured the right to proselyte freely throughout the Soviet Union.

The law specifically forbade government interference in religious activities or discrimination on the basis of religious belief. It barred government from further funding of atheistic campaigns or from financing religious activities.

Religious bodies were granted the right to own their places of worship and other property, which included the right to import literature from abroad and to publish their own literature in the country. They also received the right to engage in charitable activity and to provide religious education in public schools (after hours), as well as in their own institutions.

Parents were assured the right to bring up their children in their own religious faith. Personal income taxes for members of the clergy were made equal to that of other citizens. While income tax had been 13 percent for other Soviet citizens, the clergy had been required to pay as much as 64 percent of their personal income. This had been a long-standing Soviet policy.

The right of religious bodies to own property had already been included in the new "Law on Property Ownership," enacted by the USSR Supreme Soviet in November 1989. The USSR renewed its adherence to all of the human rights commitments of the United Nations Charter and Helsinki Process, including a statement during the final months of the existence of the Soviet Union in late 1991 that religious liberty is an "inalienable right."

The Crumbling of an Empire

Freedom of expression and participation unleashed long-suppressed national feelings among the subject peoples within the Soviet empire. It must be remembered that the Soviet Union was made up of many smaller national and ethnic groups. Some of these, such as Ukraine and the Baltic Republics, had in the past been nations in their own right. Others, as colonial peoples, developed national identity under Soviet rule. Beyond the Soviet Union were all the east-central European nations that were closely tied to the Soviet Union by diplomatic, military, and economic association.

When it was evident that, unlike previous Soviet leaders, Gorbachev would not forcibly suppress nationalist demonstrations in the German Democratic Republic, Czechoslovakia, Poland, Hungary, Romania, and Bulgaria, Communist rule collapsed quickly in these countries during 1989. The Federation of Yugoslavia also disintegrated, as did Communist rule in Albania.

The Soviet Communist Party so declined in authority and effectiveness that after March 1990, Gorbachev tended to circumvent its institutions, ruling primarily through his office as president of the USSR. By this time the leadership had recognized the right of other political parties to legally organize and participate.

Meanwhile, nationalist politics within the fifteen republics of the USSR began to follow the example of east-central Europe. Lithuania declared independence on 11 March 1990, and the Republic of Georgia on 9 April 1991. Boris Yeltsin had been freely elected president of the Russian Republic and was carrying out a strong nationalist agenda. Nationalist movements were moving toward independence in Ukraine, Moldova, Belarus, Latvia, Estonia, Transcaucasia, and the central Asian republics.

Gorbachev's Legacy

In hindsight, I believe it was providential that full freedom of religion for all faiths and commitment to international human rights provisions were accomplished before the breakup of the Soviet Union. The new nationalist states that succeeded the USSR were more concerned about restoring traditional national culture and supporting the old dominant religions. The legacy of human rights and religious equality established in the Gorbachev era could not easily be dispensed with by new states seeking international aid and recognition. The Gorbachev legislation and public policy on religious freedom provided a protection for the "nontraditional" confessions that would continue after the Soviet Union itself had passed into history.

All of the movements toward freedom of religion seemed to transpire within a very short time. It came so rapidly that many Church members were startled by the quick movement of the LDS missionary force into those countries that only a decade before had iron doors erected to kept out the gospel.

The Lord's Timetable

Since the 1970s, the leaders and general membership of The Church of Jesus Christ of Latter-day Saints have unitedly prayed in a concerted way for the Lord to open Communist lands for the preaching of the gospel of Jesus Christ. Then, when it happened so very quickly, many were astounded, not expecting to see the answer to those prayers in our lifetime.

Yet, during the brief period of what the Communist Party had considered would be its "Twelfth Five-Year Plan," (1986–1991), a revolution of freedom peacefully transformed this authoritarian society, overthrowing the party, the Soviet state, and its international empire. Miraculously, this revolution was essentially nonviolent, opening the way for 425 million people in the Soviet Union and east-central Europe to freely receive the gospel of Jesus Christ and the teachings of other faiths.

The unfolding of these dramatic events should remind us of Nephi's great testimony of the Lord: "For behold he is mightier than all the earth" (1 Nephi 4:1). The Lord has his own timetable, and when the season approaches for a great people to receive his word, all of the elaborate barriers designed by the evil one melt away like the hoarfrost before the warm rays of the sun.

Truly in our day is fulfilled the prophecy of the psalmist:

"He brought them out of darkness and the shadow of death, and brake their bands in sunder. . . .

"For he hath broken the gates of brass, and cut the bars of iron in sunder. . . .

"He sent his word, and healed them, and delivered them from their destructions.

"Oh that men would praise the Lord for his goodness, and for his wonderful works to the children of men!" (Psalm 107:14, 16, 20–21).

Chapter 4

"THY LIGHT IS COME"

"Arise, shine; for thy light is come, and the
glory of the Lord is risen upon thee."
—Isaiah 60:1

Many of the initial Russian and Estonian members of The Church of Jesus Christ of Latter-day Saints received the restored gospel while visiting abroad in Europe, and especially in Finland, during the latter 1980s. Some members of the Church in Finland taught, fellowshipped, and trained these early converts when the latter visited Finland.

In the winter of 1989–1990, President Steven R. Mecham of the Finland Helsinki Mission received authorization for some of his missionaries who had already learned Russian to visit these new Soviet members in their homes in Leningrad and Vyborg, Russia, and in Tallinn, Estonia, for a few days at a time. The missionaries would home teach and fellowship these baptized members as well as answer gospel questions of non-member friends of Soviet Latter-day Saints.

The Beginning in Russia and the Baltic States

Over the next few months, changes came rapidly because many Russians and Estonians desired to be taught and baptized. The new Finland Helsinki East Mission commenced operations on 1 July 1990, when President Gary L. Browning and his family arrived in Helsinki. His assignment was to preside over the work in Russia and the Baltic States; initially he supervised the work from mission headquarters in Finland.

37

President Browning, a prominent professor of Russian at Brigham Young University, found a total of about 175 members of the Church in Leningrad, Vyborg, Moscow, and Tallinn when he arrived. The new mission started with sixteen missionaries (see Gary L. Browning, "Out of Obscurity," pp. 676–77).

Local member-operated branches were organized in Leningrad, Vyborg, and Tallinn during 1990. For some time there had been an international branch in Moscow, but the first branch operated there by local Russian members was organized in March 1991.

Initially, missionaries entered Russia and Estonia on short-term tourist visas that had to be renewed by returning to Helsinki, Finland. In March 1991, the Church applied to the government of the Russian Republic for official registration. The official acceptance of registration by the government was announced in Moscow by Russian vice president Aleksander Rutskoi during the summer 1991 tour of the Mormon Tabernacle Choir to that city.

The Beginning in Ukraine

On 7 October 1990, two of President Browning's former missionaries now assigned to the Austria Vienna East Mission—Elders Ivan Stratov of Melbourne, Australia, and Brian Bradbury of Seattle, Washington—arrived in Kiev. This marked the official beginning of Latter-day Saint missionary work in Ukraine.

It was an exciting time for those who first entered the vast untouched area known as Ukraine. The elders, functioning as missionaries out of Austria under the able direction of President Dennis B. Neuenschwander, arrived in Kiev at the historic moment when the political breeze of freedom was everywhere in the air. Religious liberty was at stake throughout the entire Ukraine. The timing for the elders could not have been better.

The authoritarian rule of Ukrainian Communist Party first

Elder Brian Bradbury with President and Sister Biddulph.

secretary Volodymyr Shcherbitskii had ended in the fall of 1989. Shcherbitskii, an old Brezhnev protégé, had resisted Gorbachev's reforms, both in the Party Politburo in Moscow and especially in Ukraine, which he ruled with an iron fist.

Members of the Ukrainian cultural intelligentsia had appealed to Gorbachev to end Shcherbitskii's authoritarianism. In mid-September 1989, Gorbachev flew to Kiev to personally oversee the ouster of Shcherbitskii.

With the fall of Shcherbitskii, the rule of the Ukrainian Communist Party began to rapidly crumble during 1990 following the formation of "The People's Movement for Restructuring," called Rukh, which was the new Ukrainian nationalist organization. Rukh took the country by storm. In Ukraine the anticipation of freedom was everywhere.

Rukh did well in March 1990 in the first competitive parliamentary elections ever held in Ukraine, and this in spite of reported widespread Communist fraud at the polls. Of course, the old Communist Party of Ukraine made a concerted attempt to suppress Rukh, even to the extent of arresting a deputy of Parliament. But massive student demonstrations on Kreshchatik Street in Kiev on 1 October 1990, and in Parliament two weeks later, were joined by factory workers. The Communist Party

Early missionaries in Kiev meet in Provo, Utah, reunion. Front row: Cynthia Robbins, Melinda Richards, Colleen Biddulph. Back row: John Lunt, Aaron Love, Scott Suggs, Gregory Christiansen, Matthew Rowe, Quinton Spencer.

reluctantly agreed by 18 October to desist from its massive repression of Rukh and other opposition movements.

That happened eleven days after the LDS missionaries arrived in Kiev on 7 October, a time between the two great political demonstrations of October 1990. Those young elders were there to witness the end of Communist attempts to interfere with political liberty in the Ukrainian capital. It was a historical, glorious moment.

In fact, Elder Stratov conducted the first Latter-day Saint church service in Kiev, with seven investigators attending, on the very Sunday of the great student demonstrations at Parliament that erupted mere blocks from the Latter-day Saint meeting. Ironically, this first meeting of the Church had convened in the Ukrainian Writers Union Hall on Ordzhonikidze Street, located a scant fifty yards down the street from the massive headquarters building of the Communist Party Central Committee of Ukraine. This hall remained the meeting place of the Church for eighteen months.

Sister Lyubov Korolyova, district Relief Society president in Kiev (second from left), leads observance of 150th anniversary of the founding of Relief Society.

The New Law on Religious Freedom

Ukraine, as previously explained, had been particularly reluctant to grant recognition to religious confessions other than the Russian Orthodox Church during the period 1986–1990. Less than two weeks before the elders arrived in Kiev, however, the historic "Law on the Freedom of Conscience and Religious Organizations" had finally been enacted by the USSR's Supreme Soviet in Moscow on 26 September 1990 and signed by President Gorbachev. Equal protection was thereby afforded to all religions, and the right to freely proselyte was guaranteed throughout the USSR a few days before the missionaries arrived in Kiev.

The Ukrainian nationalist movement, in stark contrast to the Ukrainian Communist Party, initially embraced freedom of conscience and unfettered religious activity for all confessions. Soon a Ukrainian "Law on The Freedom of Conscience and Religious Organizations," similar to the USSR law, was enacted by the Parliament in Kiev on 23 April 1991.

As they left for Kiev, Elders Stratov and Bradbury received a list of individuals residing in that city who had been referred by acquaintances as contacts who might be willing to hear the message of the restored gospel. As it turned out, many of these individuals were not interested in studying with the missionaries; but when the elders telephoned Valery Stavichenko, he agreed to meet them at the Hotel Rus', where they were temporarily staying.

Valery Was Ready

In his personal history, Valery described his first meeting with Elders Stratov and Bradbury. It was a crisp October day. They waited for him in front of the Rus' Hotel. Valery was impressed by their physical height (Elder Bradbury standing six feet eight inches, Elder Stratov six feet five) as well as with their grooming and neat appearance, their open friendliness, and an aura of honesty and spirituality about them.

Valery was trained as an electronic engineer but had recently begun a private business venture. He and his wife, Tatyana, attended the first LDS worship service at the hall of the Ukrainian Writers Union with five other investigators. In subsequent discussions with the elders, he read the Book of Mormon and other literature given him and became convinced to accept the new faith.

Although there were several investigators preparing for baptism, the missionaries judged Valery to be the first who was fully ready to make that commitment. Valery later wrote an account of his baptism:

> I desired to be baptized in the Dnieper River. The poor young missionary accepted my caprice without complaint, and on November 25, 1990, this young man from Australia (Elder Stratov), who had never even seen snow before his mission, entered the icy waters and conducted the first ordinance of baptism of The Church of Jesus Christ of Latter-day Saints in the history of Ukraine.
>
> My first testimony I received immediately after confir-

President Valery Stavichenko, his wife, Tatyana, and their daughters. Valery was the first citizen of Ukraine to be baptized. He joined the Church on November 25, 1990.

mation. I asked, "Lord, do you accept what I am doing?" And my breast swelled unto bursting with a feeling of enormous joy and peace, insomuch that I felt physically drained of my energy. I was filled with a love for the whole world.

Valery Stavichenko was to become the first native member in Ukraine to hold the Melchizedek Priesthood and to serve as branch president in Ukraine. His wife, Tatyana, was also soon baptized, and together they went to the Freiberg Germany Temple to be endowed and sealed on the first temple excursion from Ukraine, in November 1992. Afterward their children were sealed to them, and they also became parents of the first baby in Ukraine to be born under the covenant of temple marriage. Valery was also called to organize a second branch on the Left Bank, and subsequently he was called as the first district president in Kiev.

Others Were Ready

Two other members of this first group of investigators accepting baptism were Aleksei Roms, a university student finishing his degree in chemistry, and his cousin, Aleksandr Manzhos, who was a biochemist working in the Ukrainian Academy of Sciences. Aleksei became the first elders quorum president in Ukraine and the first Ukrainian to serve a full-time mission. He fulfilled an honorable mission in the

England Manchester Mission from 1992 to 1994. In 1992 he was also the first Ukrainian to be endowed in the temple in London.

Aleksandr Manzhos served as a counselor in the first branch presidency and then became branch president when Valery Stavichenko was called to form a second branch. He later became a district president in Kiev, and on 6 April 1994 was chosen president of the National Administration of The Church of Jesus Christ of Latter-day Saints for the Republic of Ukraine, a body representing LDS Church leadership in meetings and negotiations with the government of Ukraine. By that time there were forty branches with local presidencies in two missions for all of Ukraine. Aleksandr's wife, Natalya, and daughter were baptized in 1993 and subsequently sealed to him in the temple.

The Church grew gradually until there were forty-four members in the first branch, with eight young missionaries and one missionary couple serving at the time that Colleen and I arrived in Kiev on 29 June 1991 to hold our first meetings with missionaries and members.

It was apparent to us that the work of the Lord had been firmly launched in Ukraine.

Chapter 5

"NO POWER SHALL
STAY MY HAND"

*"Whosoever I will shall go forth among all
nations, and it shall be told them what they
shall do; for I have a great work laid up in
store, for Israel shall be saved, and I will lead
them whithersoever I will, and no power shall
stay my hand."*

—Doctrine and Covenants 38:33

By 1991 the power of separatism among the main nationalities was so strong that the survival of the Soviet Union itself was in serious question. Gorbachev attempted to preserve the USSR by proposing a new "Union Treaty."

This new treaty would grant powerful authority and autonomy to the national republics under a weaker federal government, ruled jointly by a council composed of Gorbachev as USSR president and the fifteen presidents of the national republics. Even this weak federalism was very hard to sell to the nationalities.

Meanwhile, a number of Gorbachev's leading colleagues in Moscow who were alarmed at this proposal and the decline of central control determined that they must seize power to prevent the destruction of the USSR and the ruin of Socialism. The leading conspirators were Vladimir Alexandrovich Kryuchkov, chairman of the KGB (Soviet secret police); Dmitri Timofeyevich Yazov, a leading army general who was USSR minister of defense; Valentin Sergeyevich Pavlov, USSR prime minister; and Gennady Ivanovich

Yanayev, USSR Vice President (to President Gorbachev). Kryuchov was the real mastermind of the conspiracy.

In addition, the leading conspirators obtained the support of Anatoly Ivanovich Lukyanov, chairman of the USSR Supreme Soviet (the Parliament); Boris Karlovich Pugo, USSR minister of internal affairs (including supervision of regular police); Valery Ivanovich Boldin, Gorbachev's chief of staff; Oleg Dmitriyevich Baklanov, Communist Party secretary responsible for the defense industry; Alexander Ivanovich Tizyakov, head of the Association of State Enterprises; Oleg Semyonovich Shenin, Communist Party secretary responsible for personnel; and Vasily Alexandrovich Starodubtsev, head of the Peasants Union. President Gorbachev and his family were resting at their holiday home near the Black Sea, in Foros in the Crimea, when the coup began.

The Coup Begins

On Monday, 19 August 1991, the people of the USSR awoke to mass media announcements that this junta of conspirators had assumed power and was imposing a state of emergency. All political gatherings were banned, and the human rights enactments of the Gorbachev era were suspended. Meetings of the parliaments of national republics were banned for at least six months. Red Army troops were sent into Moscow and also surrounded Kiev and other capital cities of the national republics.

My wife, Colleen, was in Vienna, and I was in Kiev, visiting the sixteen missionaries serving there, when the coup began. Elder Ivan Stratov, the zone leader, and I were searching for an auditorium where Elders Boyd K. Packer and Dallin H. Oaks of the Quorum of the Twelve could speak to members of the Church and their guests on their forthcoming visit of 11–13 September.

We had secured a suitable hall on Lvov Square in the early morning of 19 August and were sitting with the director of the Hall of Artists to sign the documents and provide a finan-

Six veteran missionaries who opened the cities of Odessa, Simferopol, Kharkov, and Dnepropetrovsk in Ukraine: Elders John Lunt, Richard Davis, Russell van der Werf, Christopher Carpenter, Thomas Wright, and Gordon Roylance.

cial deposit when an aide came into the room and turned on the radio so that the three of us could hear the "Declaration of the State of Emergency" and all that it entailed. Since there was no specific mention of religious meetings, the director signed the agreement, but I thought to myself, *All human rights are rescinded. If the coup succeeds, it will mean the end to foreign missionary work in the Soviet Union and perhaps the banning of meetings of the LDS Church.*

Since the junta included the heads of the KGB, the Red Army, and the Ministry of Internal Affairs (which supervises the civilian police throughout the USSR), it appeared likely that all the resources of power were in the hands of the hard-line conspirators. The crowds on the metro and the trams were quiet, staring morosely at the floor. The feeling of gloom was palpable.

Seeking a Course of Action

I was staying at the old Lebid Hotel on Victory Square. As I returned to my room to attempt a call to the Area Presidency in Frankfurt, the ugly young men who hung around the hotel (whom I recognized from long experience as KGB toughs placed there to keep tabs on foreigners) confronted me brazenly with triumph written on their faces.

"Preacher, pray for me! Help Jesus save my soul!" One of them knelt in my path and pawed at my suit mockingly, then laughed lustily as I pushed past them. The fact that they were making no effort to hide their identity and the triumphant sneers on their faces seemed to be saying, "You are an enemy who will soon be gone!"

There was no way to get through to Frankfurt, so I determined to go to an old apartment recently purchased by the Church and wait for the missionaries to come. Missionaries had been called by Elder Stratov to meet me there.

Two of the young KGB toughs followed me openly, about ten yards behind, laughing and hooting, to the University Metro Station, where we descended the escalator down deep to the platform. I was determined not to lead them to the meeting with the missionaries, so I rode for several stops until I saw a train stopped in the station going the opposite direction. I suddenly jumped off the eastbound metro and made it onto the westbound train before the doors closed electronically.

After several stops west, I ascended to the street and immediately got onto a crowded old tram. At that time I didn't know the transportation system in Kiev well enough to discern where I was headed, but I jumped off and boarded an electric trolley that seemed to be going in the direction I felt would be the center of the city.

When I saw the fountains of October Revolution Square at the end of the number 18 trolley line, I knew that my instincts had been correct. I knew how to get to the apartment from the main metro stop on the square, and soon I arrived there to find most of the missionaries already quietly assembled, sitting on the floor because we still did not have sufficient furniture.

Elder and Sister Charles Creel, our missionary couple in Kiev, had stopped by the consulate of the United States on their way to the meeting. They learned that Kiev was surrounded by a large contingent of the Red Army, just outside the city. The U.S. State Department was urging all Americans to leave the Soviet Union as soon as possible.

I spent nearly an hour trying to get through to the Area Presidency on the apartment telephone, but to no avail. By that time the remaining missionaries had arrived, and we knelt and solemnly commenced the meeting with prayer.

The Lord's Comfort

I had not taken time to think what I should say to the missionaries to raise their spirits and could not tell them any instructions from the Area Presidency. I had been mission president for just over one month, and this was my first crisis. I opened my scriptures as I stood up to speak, hoping to find something appropriate. My scriptures opened exactly to Doctrine and Covenants, section 35, verses 24–27, which I asked them to turn to, then led them in reading:

> Keep all the commandments and covenants by which ye are bound; and I will cause the heavens to shake for your good, and Satan shall tremble and Zion shall rejoice upon the hills and flourish;
> And Israel shall be saved in mine own due time; . . . Lift up your hearts and be glad, your redemption draweth nigh.
> Fear not, little flock, the kingdom is yours until I come. Behold, I come quickly. Even so. Amen.

I realized by an overflowing manifestation of the Spirit that this scripture was the word of the Lord to us in our situation. I bore witness that this crisis was in the hands of the Lord and that Satan would have no power to end the work of the Lord at that time in that country. "The Lord is able to shake the heavens for our good," I told them. "Zion shall rejoice and flourish here, and Israel shall be saved in Ukraine. We need not fear."

I asked them not to wear their name tags and to return to their apartments as individual companionships, not all walking together. They were told to pack one suitcase with their most essential things and have it ready to go immediately.

49

During the crisis they could go to appointments already made but otherwise were to stay in their apartments. Every night and every morning the missionaries from the two missionary districts of Kiev were to call their district leaders, who would report to the zone leader, and he to me, that all was well.

They asked if scheduled baptisms could be performed that week in the Dnieper River, which runs through Kiev. My immediate reaction was to say no, but the Spirit seemed to say, "Yes, if you are careful and can do so unobtrusively." Eight persons were baptized in the river that historic week, one for each missionary companionship.

There were fewer than sixty members of the Church in Ukraine at that time and only three men ordained to the Melchizedek Priesthood. I interviewed several other worthy brethren and ordained them elders in the Melchizedek Priesthood so they would have sufficient authority if the missionaries had to be temporarily withdrawn from Kiev. We discussed how they would function, and they promised with emotion to be true to the gospel and the Church. Several older adult sisters begged me to allow them to hide the missionaries in their apartments. "We are ready to risk prison, even our lives, that the gospel may go forth. We must not lose the blessing of the priesthood," they implored. "Please do not take the missionaries away from us!"

I explained to them that we would remain in Kiev if officially permitted, but we would not stay without legal permission. Then I promised them that through the power given their Ukrainian brethren, the Lord's work would continue and flourish in Kiev, no matter what happened, if they would keep the commandments, follow their appointed spiritual leaders, seek for personal revelation, and obey their governmental authorities. They promised to do so. It was a poignant meeting, attended by the Spirit and by the expression of many tender feelings for one another.

The Coup Failed: The Role of a Future Mormon

The Ukrainian Parliament refused to disband as the junta in Moscow demanded. I wondered if the Red Army troops encircling Kiev would attack and occupy the city. With Elder Creel's shortwave radio we listened to the BBC broadcast in London and learned of the events in Moscow. We were also able to call missionaries in Moscow (part of the Helsinki East Mission under President Gary L. Browning) and learn of their circumstances, but we were unable to reach the outside world.

For two nights I listened to the truck convoys crossing Victory Square. I could see the headquarters building of Rukh, the Ukrainian nationalist organization, across the street. Instead of the official Ukrainian Soviet flag, it flew the blue and gold flag of Ukrainian independence. When awakened in the middle of the night by the truck convoys, I would look outside to see if the flag was still fluttering in the light of the square. Seeing the flag, I knew there had not yet been a Soviet occupation of the Ukrainian capitol, and I would go back to sleep.

On my second day at the mission apartment, a phone call came through from the Creels' daughter who lives in Las Vegas, where it would have been the middle of the night. I asked her to call Elder Hans B. Ringger in Frankfurt and my wife in Vienna to report that we were all well and planning to stay in Kiev unless the Brethren decided that we must leave.

Miraculously, she got through again ten minutes later to report that she had completed the calls I had requested and that Elder Ringger confirmed that it was correct to remain in Kiev and do all that I had instructed the missionaries to do. He had been trying to reach us from Frankfurt, but only Las Vegas succeeded—twice! The operator told the Creels' daughter that she must have some special connections "above" to get through twice in ten minutes.

I returned to the Hotel Lebid to find that CNN Television had been set up in the lobby, showing Russian president Boris

Former military officer
Vasily Lubarets,
his wife, Lidia, and
their three daughters,
Tatyana, Darya,
and Nastya.

Nikolayevich Yeltsin and his brave supporters in Moscow defying the tanks. All the hotel employees and guests were watching and cheering. The menacing KGB toughs had all mysteriously disappeared from the hotel.

It was apparent that the coup was unraveling. A key reason was that Red Army colonels and majors who had been commanded by the generals to attack the crowds protecting the Russian White House in Moscow bravely refused to lead their men to attack citizens. One of these brave senior officers was Vasily Lubarets, a Ukrainian who would later be baptized into the Church in Kiev. He was assigned to the USSR General Staff in Moscow and was required to explain to junior officers under his command the plan of attack. He has written an account of this event:

> If I were to fulfill the command given me, I would never be able to forgive myself in the future, for our army has never attacked defenseless citizens. On the other hand, if I told the junior officers the truth, I would risk the lives of my wife, my daughters, and myself.
>
> I understood clearly that I had to make a choice and that time would not wait for me, . . . so I said to the junior offi-

cers the following: "A coup has been committed in the country. The putschers have grabbed power, and they are criminals. They will give you weapons and orders to shoot at people, but remember that there are soldiers in places where your children, mothers, and wives are, and those soldiers could get the same orders, too."

"What shall we do?" they asked me. "If we do not fulfill the orders, they will kill us!" "Yes, they will kill us, but it is better to be a victim than a killer." These were my last words to the formation. Later there were two sleepless nights near the radio; then there was the victory of the unarmed people upon the tanks. There were lists in the Party Military Department with the names of people who had to be arrested, and my name was there, too. They began to arrest worthy officers in other divisions. Finally, after waiting three days and two nights, common sense and the law won in this country.

The brave colonels and majors like Vasily Lubarets, and some courageous generals too, saved the Soviet Union from a disaster like Tiannanmen Square in China and helped defeat the coup of the junta in Moscow. Vasily Lubarets learned only later, after his baptism in Kiev into The Church of Jesus Christ of Latter-day Saints, that his bravery had also helped to save the opportunity for him, his family, and his people to receive the restored gospel of Jesus Christ.

The Lord's Miracle

On the third day of the attempted coup, it was clear to all the crowds assembled in the center of Kiev on October Revolution Square, soon to be named "Independence Square," that the coup had miraculously failed. I wanted to be in this rejoicing crowd, but I had forbidden the missionaries to be in political demonstrations, so I felt that I must set an example and keep my distance. But old men ran past me shouting: "Thanks be to God; we are free! Thanks be to God for our freedom!"

All the missionaries assembled again at the mission

apartment on the third day, 21 August. We'd all come to the testimony meeting fasting with thanksgiving before the Lord, rejoicing that our mission would continue. Our tall, Russian-Australian zone leader, Elder Ivan Stratov, stood up and recited with deep power and feeling, from perfect memory, the words of the Prophet Joseph Smith:

"The Standard of Truth has been erected; no unhallowed hand can stop the work from progressing; persecutions may rage, mobs may combine, armies may assemble, calumny may defame, but the truth of God will go forth boldly, nobly, and independent, till it has penetrated every continent, visited every clime, swept every country, and sounded in every ear, till the purposes of God shall be accomplished, and the Great Jehovah shall say the work is done" (Joseph Smith, *History of the Church*, 4:540).

No one felt that he had been melodramatic. Tears of gratitude and resolve streamed down our faces as we heard him charge us to show our thanks to the Lord by serving with all our heart, might, mind, and strength. No one who was there will ever forget those electrifying words of the Prophet Joseph delivered from the very soul of a great young servant of the Lord with a thick Aussie accent.

I read to them from section 1 of the Doctrine and Covenants, verse 5: "And they shall go forth and none shall stay them, for I the Lord have commanded them." I also read section 38, verse 33, with them: "Whosoever I will shall go forth among all nations, and it shall be told them what they shall do; for I have a great work laid up in store, for Israel shall be saved, and I will lead them whithersoever I will, and no power shall stay my hand."

We knew that we had witnessed a miracle of the Lord. "For behold, he is mightier than all the earth, then why not mightier than [the ministers of state and the generals and the KGB, who have conspired to deny the freedom of the people to hear his word]?" (1 Nephi 4:1).

We rejoiced in testimony together in acknowledgement of

the great good brought about by the hand of the Lord. We recommitted to give our whole souls to him in obedience and service, that his great future harvest in Ukraine would, indeed, come to pass. It was a sacred day, never to be forgotten.

The End of the USSR

USSR's President Gorbachev returned on 22 August, as he remarked, "to a different world" from that which he had left. Yeltsin, the president of the Russian Republic, was the great hero of the country, and Gorbachev played less and less of a central role as events developed. The coup had failed, but its defeat had effectively destroyed any further allegiance to the central government.

On 20 August, Estonia declared its independence. The next day Latvia followed suit. Ukraine declared independence on 24 August, Belarus on 25 August, Moldova on 27 August, Azerbaijan on 30 August, and Kirgizstan and Uzbekistan on 31 August. Taikistan declared independence on 9 September, Armenia on 23 September, and Turkmenistan on 27 October. This left only Russia and Kazakhstan in the Soviet Union, and with the power clearly in the hands of the two republic presidents, Boris Yeltsin and Nursultan Nazarbayev, rather than Mikhail Gorbachev.

Gorbachev continued to try to put the union back together in some kind of loose system, but particularly Ukraine's failure to cooperate with these plans led to the final breakdown of the Union of Soviet Socialist Republics. Gorbachev resigned on 25 December, and on 31 December the USSR ceased to be. The greatest territorial empire in the world, which Russian tsars and Soviet Communists had taken five hundred years to gather into one state, was gone with one stroke of Gorbachev's pen!

President Yeltsin outlawed the Communist Party in Russia due to its central role in the abortive coup. The presidents of the other new successor republics followed suit and abolished the Party, which had once ruled with absolute power throughout this great Eurasian subcontinent. Many former Communists, however, survived in new political movements and in some cases again occupied positions of political leadership in the new republics. (After a ruling by the Constitutional Court of Russia in November 1992, new communist parties were allowed to organize in the Russian Federation. The new Russian Communist Party has become one of the major opponents of President Yeltsin.)

Gorbachev, a Modern Cyrus

A few days before Gorbachev's resignation as president of the USSR, I had a long talk with a Baptist minister named Ivan Medvedev in Donetsk about the historical role of Mikhail Gorbachev. We agreed that he would be regarded in history as both a tragic and a heroic figure. A person of great intelligence, civility, and ability, he was nevertheless not able to reform and save either Communism or the Soviet Union as an empire of nations. His economic initiatives were implemented too slowly and tentatively and failed miserably. He ended his six-year period on the world stage not only despised by Communist hard-liners but also rejected by the overwhelming majority of the citizenry that had originally taken hope in his program and promises.

We agreed, nevertheless, that Gorbachev would be remembered as one who brought human rights—especially freedom of expression and freedom of religion—to the Soviet peoples. We agreed that, in biblical terms, Gorbachev was the "Cyrus" of the Slavic peoples and other captive nations. Pastor Medvedev expressed the conviction that "Gorbachev was the Cyrus whom God called to permit a great captive people to return and build the spiritual walls of Zion in this country!"

I heartily agreed and still agree.

Chapter 6

"THE MORNING BREAKS"

*"The morning breaks, the shadows flee; Lo,
Zion's standard is unfurled!"*

—*Hymns*, no. 1

At the beginning of the twentieth century, leaders of The Church of Jesus Christ of Latter-day Saints were hoping to receive approval from the tsarist government to introduce the restored gospel into the Russian Empire. To this end, Elder Francis M. Lyman of the Council of the Twelve Apostles and president of the European Mission visited the capital city of St. Petersburg and offered a prayer of dedication on 6 August 1903. This hope was not to be realized for an additional eighty-seven years.

The Dedication of Russia and Armenia

St. Petersburg was renamed Leningrad during the Soviet era. When missionary work was able to commence in Leningrad, Elder Russell M. Nelson of the Quorum of the Twelve Apostles offered a special prayer of gratitude and rededication in that city on 26 April 1990. In Moscow during the Mormon Tabernacle Choir's tour, Elder Nelson and Elder Dallin H. Oaks went to a park near the Kremlin walls on 25 June 1991, where Elder Nelson offered a blessing on the people of the Soviet Union. On the previous day, 24 June, Elder Oaks and Elder Nelson, accompanied by Elder Hans B. Ringger of the Seventy and president of the Europe Area, had gathered with others in a brief ceremony to bless and dedicate the Republic of Armenia. Elder Oaks offered a prayer in Yerevan, at a site in view of Mount Ararat (see "Two Republics in USSR Are Dedicated," p. 3).

Recognition of the Church in Kiev

When Colleen and I first arrived in Kiev in 1991, we learned that The Church of Jesus Christ of Latter-day Saints was not yet officially registered. Members of the Church had already met in April in the prescribed way to petition the government for official recognition. They had sent this application to the city administration of Kiev with the help of a noted Ukrainian lawyer and jurist, Vasily Kisil, who was employed to assist the Church.

In early August 1991, there still was no word from the government on our application. We were already planning for a September visit to Kiev by two Apostles from the headquarters of the Church in Salt Lake City: Elder Boyd K. Packer and Elder Dallin H. Oaks. I was hoping that they might be coming to offer a dedicatory prayer for the Church and a blessing for the people of Ukraine, but I was afraid this might not happen if the Church was not officially recognized by the government before their arrival.

Dr. Kisil assured me that everything possible was being done to secure official registration, yet he had been unsuccessful in obtaining any answer to the application. Colleen and I, with our zone leader, Elder Stratov, then went to the Lord with the prayer that somehow the Church's petition to the government might receive a positive response before the arrival of the Brethren on 11 September.

The next day was fast Sunday in Kiev, and one of the curious visitors who attended Church services was a man who introduced himself to me as Viktor Cherinko, a deputy of the City Soviet (the legislative assembly for Kiev). As a legislator, he chaired important legislative committees in the fields of economic development and environmental protection.

Mr. Cherinko had heard of the Mormons and had a favor-

In Kiev, Ukraine, missionaries gather at spot where Elder Boyd K. Packer dedicated Ukraine, September 12, 1991.

able opinion of the Church, welcoming us as a positive new element in the Kiev community. I explained to him our desire for the city government to act quickly on our application for official registration. He promised to help.

After the August political coup had failed, Mr. Cherinko introduced directly into the assembly a bill to officially register "The Kiev Community of The Church of Jesus Christ of Latter-day Saints." This bill was passed by the City Soviet at midnight on 9 September 1991, two days before the arrival of Elder Packer, Elder Oaks, and Elder Dennis B. Neuenschwander, who as a member of the Seventy was serving as second counselor in the Europe Area Presidency.

The Dedication Site

On 10 September, Colleen and I prayerfully visited a number of parks and inspirational view points in Kiev. In case Elder Packer was coming to dedicate Ukraine, and just in case we might be asked to suggest a site, I wanted to be prepared with one or more proposals.

We walked up the trail through the forest to the statue of Prince Vladimir ("Volodymyr" in Ukrainian) on a beautiful vantage point high above the Dnieper River and the central part of Kiev. We had looked at several other places, but both of us instantly felt a wonderful feeling that, if asked, we would

59

recommend this site. If we were not asked for a suggestion, however, we would say nothing.

Vladimir was the Grand Prince of Kiev who was converted to Christianity and then oversaw the baptism of the inhabitants of the whole city in the Dnieper River in 988. This was the official beginning of the reception of Christianity by the ancestors of the Russian, Ukrainian, and Belarussian people.

The huge statue depicts Vladimir in the attitude of prayer, his eyes upward as he holds aloft a cross. It is a very peaceful, beautiful, and spiritual spot. The statue was erected in the middle of the nineteenth century, and I am unaware of any other public religious statues, apart from those in churches, that survived the seventy-year rule of Communism. Somehow this one did.

The Dedication of Ukraine

The Brethren arrived on 11 September, and I reported to them the successful registration of the Church. Elder Packer declared that he had received the assignment from the First Presidency to offer a dedicatory prayer and asked if we would like to show him some possible spots where it might be done. The first place we took the Brethren was to the Vladimir statue, and Elder Packer immediately declared that it was the right place.

At 6:00 A.M. on 12 September 1991, twenty missionaries serving in Kiev, about twenty members of the Church, Colleen, and I accompanied Elders Packer, Oaks, and Neuenschwander to the Vladimir statue.

Some of the members were confused about the location and started down a walk toward another park, not far from the correct spot. A total stranger stopped them, saying: "You are going the wrong way. The Mormon gathering is at the Vladimir statue." This seemed strange because we did not publicly announce the dedication. Those invited had been instructed to keep the meeting private.

I was asked to conduct this historic service, which commenced about 7:00 A.M. with the singing of the hymn "Joseph Smith's First Prayer" (*Hymns,* no. 26), followed by an opening prayer offered by branch president Valery Stavichenko. Elder Oaks and Elder Neuenschwander spoke briefly; then Elder Packer delivered the dedicatory prayer.

Elder Packer's prophetic blessing included the poetic words of an earlier latter-day Apostle, Parley P. Pratt:

> The morning breaks, the shadows flee;
> Lo, Zion's standard is unfurled!
> The dawning of a brighter day,
> The dawning of a brighter day
> Majestic rises on the world.
>
> The clouds of error disappear
> Before the rays of truth divine;
> The glory bursting from afar,
> The glory bursting from afar
> Wide o'er the nations soon will shine.
>
> The Gentile fulness now comes in,
> And Israel's blessings are at hand.
> Lo, Judah's remnant, cleansed from sin,
> Lo, Judah's remnant, cleansed from sin,
> Shall in their promised Canaan stand.
>
> Jehovah speaks! Let earth give ear,
> And Gentile nations turn and live.
> His mighty arm is making bare,
> His mighty arm is making bare
> His cov'nant people to receive.
>
> Angels from heav'n and truth from earth
> Have met, and both have record borne;
> Thus Zion's light is bursting forth,
> Thus Zion's light is bursting forth
> To bring her ransomed children home.
>
> —"The Morning Breaks," *Hymns,* no. 1

It was a gray, cloudy morning with intermittent showers. As Elder Packer's prophetic dedicatory prayer came to an end, however, members of the assembled group opened their eyes to see a brief parting of the heavy black clouds. Rays of the early-morning sun were shining magnificently on the river and on the city below, as if to proclaim: "The morning breaks on Ukraine; the shadows flee. Lo, Zion's standard is unfurled in this ancient land!" Then, after a moment, the sun was gone and heavy clouds and showers remained throughout the day.

It was also deeply symbolic that the Apostles witnessed workmen on "Independence Square" start to remove the giant statue of Lenin on that same day, 12 September. Elder Packer commented that Prince Vladimir had removed the ancient idol of Perun from Kiev at the time that Christianity was received, and the removal of the modern idol of Lenin signified that the people were ready to receive the fulness of the gospel.

That evening Elders Packer, Oaks, and Neuenschwander spoke to a capacity crowd at the five-hundred-seat auditorium of the Hall of Artists on Lvov Square. Almost all of the seventy-five members of the Church in Kiev were in attendance, and many of the four hundred nonmembers present were visibly touched by the Spirit.

Many who were there that night for the first time were baptized in the coming weeks and months. The dedication of the Republic of Ukraine and the testimony of living Apostles of Jesus Christ were the beginning point of an amazing spiritual harvest.

Beginning and Registration in Other Ukrainian Cities

In November 1991, I was given the assignment to visit several cities in Ukraine, southern Russia, and Moldova in order to investigate living conditions and the people's receptivity toward our missionaries. Elder Ivan Stratov accompanied me on the visit to four eastern Ukrainian cities and four cities of the Russian North Caucasus during the last week of November and first nine days of December. Elder Brian Bradbury accompanied me on a visit to Kishinev, Moldova, and several cities of southern Ukraine and the Crimea at the end of December and early January 1992.

We were hospitably received by both public officials and ordinary citizens in most of the cities we visited, but especially in Donetsk and Kharkov. On the night of 26 November in Donetsk, I dreamed of a future stake of Zion in that city and a Latter-day Saint meetinghouse on a beautiful green site. I also dreamed that Ricks College would perform some kind of significant mission in Donetsk.

Elder Stratov and I also visited Rostov-on-the-Don, Krasnodar, Sochi, and Novorossisk in the Russian North Caucasus and had a strong positive feeling about the future missionary potential of that area. These cities would compose the future Russia Rostov Mission on 1 July 1994.

In March 1992, we received approval for missionaries to go to Donetsk. On Wednesday morning, 18 March, four missionaries arrived by train in this hub city of the Donbas Coal Basin. Leading the group of four was Elder Gregory Christiansen; the others included Elders Robin Curtis, Gregory Rossiter, and Rory Allen. They immediately met with and were welcomed by local government officials, including the State Council for Religious Affairs, establishing a cordial relationship.

The missionaries found a number of their early converts in Donetsk among members of the world-famous Donbas Ukrainian Dancers and Choir, who had performed at Ricks College and had lived in the homes of Latter-day Saints in Rexburg, Idaho. They had also hosted their former Rexburg hosts in Donetsk during 1990 and as a result had received copies of the Book of Mormon, tracts, and LDS pictures. They were ready to receive the missionaries with open arms.

By November there was a sizable congregation of Latter-day Saints with local leaders who applied for formal registration of the Church in Donetsk. A branch in nearby Gorlovka also applied for registration at the same time. In May 1993, official registration of the Church in Donetsk and Gorlovka

Some of the early missionaries in Donetsk, Ukraine: Elders Christiansen, Suggs, Harris, and Curtis.

was approved. By this time there were four branches in Donetsk, with local officers directing all activities, and branches were functioning in nearby Makayevka as well as in Gorlovka.

The leadership of the Donetsk city government offered the Church a beautiful site for a future chapel to be erected. The Church accepted the offer. In the fall of 1993, Ricks College professors Robert Schwartz and Robert Markham, along with their families, accepted the college's invitation to donate a year of teaching English and religion at a new private university in Donetsk. This initiative generated a tremendous spirit of goodwill for the Church in Donetsk.

Elder Christopher Carpenter was called to lead a group of four elders to open Kharkov (the second largest city in Ukraine) at the end of September 1992. The others chosen were Elders Russell van der Werf, Edward Quinlan, and Kendall Simpson. The missionaries found that a number of people were already spiritually prepared, and the Church grew rapidly in that city. By 1 July 1993, there were seven local branches in Kharkov, which were assigned to the new Ukraine Donetsk Mission. Official registration of the Church in Kharkov was not granted until after the division of the mission.

On Saturday, 8 May 1993, twelve missionaries departed to open three additional Ukrainian cities: Odessa, Dnepropetrovsk, and Simferopol. Elder John Lunt led the missionaries of the Odessa group, which included Elders Gordon Roylance, Ryan Gibby, and Curtis Bingham. Elder Christopher Carpenter led the Dnepropetrovsk group, which included Elders Russell van der Werf, Timothy Lunt, and Cory Clegg. Elder Richard Davis led the Simferopol group, which included Elders Thomas Wright, Brandon Arrington, and Jesus Condori (of Peru).

In all three cities there were a number of people already spiritually prepared to receive the restored gospel, as had been the case in Donetsk and Kharkov. For example, eleven accepted the commitment to be baptized in Odessa during the missionaries' first week there. In Simferopol a university professor of theology had finished reading the Book of Mormon—and had been converted by it—just a few days before the elders arrived.

The Church in Odessa grew rapidly during 1993 and 1994 and achieved official registration in December 1993. The Church in Simferopol also steadily developed, receiving official registration by the government of Crimea in November 1993. In Dnepropetrovsk there were also many converts. Six weeks after the opening, however, the missionaries in this city were assigned to the jurisdiction of the new Ukraine Donetsk Mission.

After appealing the denial of registration in Kharkov, the Church was finally officially registered there in February 1994. With the Church registered in Kiev, Donetsk, Kharkov, Odessa, Simferopol, and Gorlovka, and pending applications in Dnepropetrovsk and Makayevka, the Latter-day Saints were entitled to apply for the registration of a national center for the Church, which was officially proposed to the government of Ukraine on 6 April 1994.

The opening and dedication of Belarus in Minsk. Front row: Elder Karl Borcherding, Sister Hannah Borcherding, Sister Colleen Biddulph, President Howard L. Biddulph, Sister Dantzel Nelson, Elder Russell M. Nelson, Sister Helen Ringger, Elder Hans B. Ringger. Back row: Some of the full-time missionaries serving in Belarus.

Anatoly and the Beginning in Belarus

The story of the beginning of The Church of Jesus Christ of Latter-day Saints in Belarus is a classic example of how the Lord prepares key people in advance to help establish the gospel in new lands.

In January 1993, I received word that the First Presidency and the Council of the Twelve had authorized Elder Karl Borcherding of Hanover, Germany, and his wife, Hanna, to go to Minsk, Belarus, to help prepare that country for the opening of the restored gospel in the Republic of Belarus. I was assigned to take them to Minsk and to help them become well established there.

Elder and Sister Borcherding did not speak Russian or Belarussian and had never lived in Russia or Belarus. I had never visited Minsk and had no contacts there (or so I thought). They would be arriving 20 January 1993, the coldest period of the winter there.

How shall I get them established in Minsk, given such circumstances? I wondered. Then I remembered Anatoly. Anatoly had been writing to me from Minsk for more than a year. He was a convert to a Protestant evangelical group from the United States and believed he had been saved. Yet he was

Elder Russell M. Nelson of the Quorum of the Twelve visits with Anatoly Neverov, who before his baptism helped prepare the way for the Church in Belarus.

very curious about the Book of Mormon and the Latter-day Saints. A graduate of the Institute of Foreign Languages in Minsk, he worked in the travel industry.

Although I had a missionary who handled referrals, for some reason I had decided to deal with this one myself. I sent Anatoly a copy of the Book of Mormon and other literature. He read them carefully and asked many deep questions by return letters. One time it took me nine single-spaced, typed pages to answer all of his questions adequately.

I kept wondering why I was spending time personally on this case when there were so many other things demanding my efforts. Besides, I reasoned, he still believes he is a saved evangelical and lives where there are no missionaries serving. But a feeling inside of me kept telling me that it was important for me to continue this personal relationship. In the course of time we established close ties.

While pondering how to help the Borcherdings become established in Minsk, I suddenly remembered Anatoly. I telephoned him and asked if he would meet us on 20 January and help us look for an apartment for them. He was very willing to help and succeeded in locating a lovely apartment.

He did not speak German, and Elder Borcherding did not speak Russian, but they both spoke good English, so they could communicate effectively. Anatoly took the Borcherdings shopping regularly, acquainted them with the city transportation system, and introduced them to many friends. He also arranged visas. Every day he went out with Elder Borcherding to meet people—ordinary people on the street as well as prominent government officials—thus becoming his translator and indispensable helper. Through this means more than thirty people became interested in hearing about the Church during a period of thirty days. These people would later be taught by members of the Church fluent in Russian.

Anatoly was severely chastised by his local evangelical church for helping the Mormons. Western evangelists were paying his livelihood for helping them and threatened to fire him if he did not stop helping the Mormons. Anatoly prayed about it and received a remarkable spiritual impression from the Lord to continue to help the Mormons, even if his own church cut off his salary and membership. For this decision he was fired by the evangelists and disciplined by his church.

In early March 1993, Elder Matt Ericson, accompanied by Elders Cody Hill, Daniel Reneau, and Lyubomir Traikov (from Bulgaria), arrived in Minsk. They were there to conduct a humanitarian project but were brought into contact with many people interested in hearing about the LDS Church, including those whom the Borcherdings and Anatoly had met.

Two of the early converts became presidents of the first two branches in Minsk: Yuri, a lawyer, and Mikhail, an architect. Anatoly made the decision to be baptized in the fall and was ordained an elder in the summer of 1994. His wife, Alla, and two children were not yet ready for such a step.

The Apostolic Dedication of Belarus

On 10 May 1993, Colleen and I met Elder Russell M. Nelson of the Quorum of the Twelve Apostles; his wife,

Belarussian Television correspondent announces the registration of the Church in Minsk and interviews Latter-day Saint leaders.

Dantzel; Elder Hans B. Ringger of the Seventy, president of the Europe Area; and his wife, Helen, at Minsk International Airport. That evening, at a public meeting in Minsk, Elder Nelson, Elder Ringger, and I spoke to a group of more than 450 people about the restored gospel of Jesus Christ.

Elder Nelson closed his powerful sermon with an apostolic testimony of Jesus Christ, delivered with perfect pronunciation in the Russian tongue.

At the close of the meeting, many people surrounded us and asked questions for an additional hour. More than two hundred people left us their names and addresses, requesting to hear more about The Church of Jesus Christ of Latter-day Saints.

Early the next day, 11 May 1993, on a beautiful, clear spring morning, Elder and Sister Nelson, Elder and Sister Ringger, Colleen and I, two couples from Kiev, and twelve others from Minsk (including the Borcherdings and Brother Anatoly) met at Yanka Kupala Park in the center of the capital city of Minsk for an apostolic blessing of dedication for Belarus.

Elder Nelson found the spot under some beautiful trees behind the museum, not far from the river. A large rock formed the center place for the service, and we gathered around it. At 7:00 A.M. these twenty-two people were alone in this beautiful park, except for the birds that were singing. Elder Nelson declared that the symbol of the birds' singing was important and was something Apostles listened for in choosing a place of dedication.

The service commenced at 7:15 A.M. with Elder Ringger giving some introductory remarks, after which I was asked to offer the invocation. Then Elder Nelson offered the dedicatory prayer. The *Church News* of June 12, 1993, reported the following:

> In the prayer of dedication, Elder Nelson prayed: "May this be the dawning of a new day. May this be a hinge-point in history, that the full potential of this country and its heroic people may be realized."
>
> He expressed gratitude for those who have been searching for truth and happiness, and prayed there might be "a rich harvest of souls" who can come unto Christ. Further in the prayer he said: "This land is rich with the blood of Israel. Let that choice lineage be gathered here and find refuge and strength in stakes of Zion. As thy children learn and obey thy commandments, let them prosper in this land."
>
> He invoked blessings upon the nation's leaders, on their righteous endeavors, and upon the country as a haven of peace, a sanctuary of faith. ("Four European Nations Dedicated," p. 6)

As in Ukraine after Elder Packer's prayer of dedication, Elder Nelson's inspired prayer of dedication and apostolic testimony in the public meeting brought the dawn of a rapid development of The Church of Jesus Christ of Latter-day Saints in Minsk. Many who had attended the public meeting were baptized into the Church. A number of these shared their new faith with family members and friends. Soon there were four branches led by local leaders in Minsk.

Colleen composed the following poem in her personal journal to remember this significant occasion:

Song of Dedication

Yes, the birds were singing
On the morn of that day!
God provided a choir
In that land far away.
A symbol of gladness,
Yea, the heavens rejoice!
Lost children of Israel
Have been granted free choice.
Now the gospel is preached,
Because One "turned the key."
Belarus, thou art blessed,
So the birds sang for thee.

—Colleen C. Biddulph, 12 May 1994

In mid-January 1994 the government of Belarus officially registered the Church in Minsk. Elder Dennis B. Neuenschwander and I, together with branch presidents Ustin and Komarov, were interviewed for "prime time" Belarussian television on the day of official registration. We were able to introduce 10.5 million Belarussian viewers to the restored gospel. Even the colored illustrations in the Book of Mormon were shown by the television camera. Ironically, it was on the exact day of the terrible Los Angeles earthquake, 17 January 1994, that this bright new day dawned for the Church and gospel of Jesus Christ in Belarus.

Chapter 7

"HEAR HEAVEN'S VOICE"

*"Hark, all ye nations! Hear heaven's voice
Thru ev'ry land that all may rejoice!"*
—*Hymns,* no. 264

Natasha and Valery were completing their postgraduate university education in Moscow. Natasha was finishing her candidate of sciences degree (Ph.D.) in preparation for her goal to become a professor of Russian and Ukrainian languages. Her husband, Valery, in preparation for the Soviet diplomatic service, was completing a similar advanced degree at the prestigious Institute of International Relations of the USSR Council of Ministers. He was preparing to become a professional economist specializing on Vietnam and Southeast Asia.

As recounted in chapter two, Natasha and Valery were among those members of the Soviet intelligentsia who began a serious search for religious values in the latter 1980s. In Moscow, Natasha was invited to attend meetings at a small branch of The Church of Jesus Christ of Latter-day Saints. She attended once or twice and looked briefly at the Book of Mormon, but she was too involved in her academic work to undertake a serious investigation of the Church.

When her candidate of sciences degree was completed, Natasha was invited by a friend and academic colleague to go to Kiev, where there were university teaching opportunities available. Valery, who had already given up his objective of a diplomatic career because the very existence of the Soviet Union was in serious question, accepted work with an

72

Kiev Church leaders with Natasha and Valery Getmanenko (center), who prepared Ukrainian translation of temple ordinances.

international private firm in Kiev. So it was that this Ukrainian couple moved to Kiev with their son, Stanislaus.

When they arrived in Kiev, Natasha learned with surprise that her longtime friend and colleague, Galina, had become a Latter-day Saint. Galina and her colleague Viktoria, a professor at Kiev University, had been invited to teach language to the Kiev missionaries each week on their preparation day. Natasha was one of the instructors whom Galina and Viktoria chose to help them teach the missionaries.

Natasha helped a group of missionaries improve their Russian conversation skills and their oral presentation of the six standard gospel discussions. In this teaching process, the missionaries helped her to understand the basic gospel principles being discussed.

Natasha and Valery Accept the Gospel

The missionaries made a deep impact on Natasha. She had never met such wonderful, spiritual young men and women. She also learned to understand more clearly the basic principles of the teachings of the Church. When one of the missionaries, Elder Matt Ericson, invited her and Valery to hear the gospel discussions, she readily accepted. She read the Book

73

of Mormon in Russian, and Valery read it in English. Both were deeply impressed by the Spirit and received testimonies of the gospel.

Valery, Natasha, and Stanislaus were baptized in February 1992. Valery became an elder later that year, and the entire family was sealed together for eternity in the Jordan River Temple in Utah during a visit to Salt Lake City in 1993.

Valery would become a translator and interpreter for the Church, especially during General Authority visits of Apostles and members of the Seventy. He was also a secretary to the mission presidency in Kiev. In January 1994, he was appointed to the International Physical Facilities Department of the Church in the Moscow office, overseeing projects in European Russia, Siberia, Ukraine, and Belarus.

Natasha served as the mission's Young Women president, organizing the youth program throughout the fifteen branches in Kiev, as well as the first all-Ukraine youth conference for 375 participants from four cities in 1993. Returning with Valery to Moscow in 1994, she became a university professor of Russian in Moscow. Valery and Natasha were invited by Church leaders to translate all of the temple ordinances into Ukrainian, a project they completed in visits to Salt Lake City during 1993 and 1994.

Slava and Zoya Find Their Spiritual Home

Vyacheslav (Slava) is a prominent Ukrainian nuclear physicist who is a department head of a prestigious nuclear physics institute of the Ukrainian government in Kiev. His wife, Zoya, is a teacher of English at a school attended by children of Ukrainian government leaders. She is also an outstanding translator.

Like many other members of the intelligentsia, Slava and Zoya experienced the spiritual crisis accompanying the collapse of Communism in the Soviet Union and the search for new religious values. Since they are Jews by nationality, it was logical for them to begin their search by going back to the synagogues of Judaism and to the Holy Torah. As described in chapter two, their journey of spiritual discovery went from Judaism to Baha'i to Protestant evangelical Christianity, and on to Catholicism. They did not feel at home spiritually in any of those religions.

The three-year search of Slava and Zoya for their spiritual home came to glorious fruition in the fall and early winter of 1991, in quite an unexpected way. The special English language program in which Zoya taught had a "Club of International Friendship," which corresponded with children from many countries of the world.

When she became club director, Zoya noticed an unanswered letter in the files from a school in Riverton, Utah, which was dated two years earlier. She decided to answer this letter. This led to a correspondence between students in Kiev and Riverton.

One of the girls from Riverton, Utah, sent a copy of a pamphlet on Joseph Smith and the Church to her Kiev pen pal. This girl took the pamphlet to Zoya, who took it home to show her husband, Slava, and their daughter, Kira. They had never heard of Mormons and found the pamphlet very interesting.

Then one evening in October 1991, after Slava had completed his scientific work for the day, Zoya and he were returning home when they noticed a small handmade announcement on a bridge near their home. The notice invited the public to meetings of The Church of Jesus Christ of Latter-day Saints on Sunday at 11:00 A.M. The address was of a drama theater very close to their home. Zoya remembered the pamphlet from Utah and persuaded Slava to go with her to meetings the following Sunday.

The Kiev Left Bank Branch was just newly organized, having first been part of the Kiev Central Branch. In the intermission after sacrament service, Slava and Zoya decided to leave, but a young missionary introduced himself and asked if he and his companion might come to their home to tell them more about the Church. Slava writes: "To refuse would have been embarrassing to us, especially when we considered how Elder [John] Lunt looked at us with such warm, friendly eyes, which radiated such love and desire to help us."

Elder Lunt and Elder Brian Bradbury visited the home of Slava and Zoya a day or two later. Slava writes:

> The first discussion did not make a strong impression upon us, but we decided to continue meeting with the missionaries and to attend church. The more we attended church and listened to the lessons of our missionaries, the closer we came to God, and imperceptibly the love of Christ began to fill our hearts, but we still were not ready to accept the invitation to become members of the Church.
>
> The missionaries counseled us to come to the swimming pool and see how the ordinance of baptism is conducted. And when we observed the baptism, then I suddenly knew perfectly and precisely that we would be baptized, that this Church is true—that this is our Church, that God desired this of us, and that we ought to fulfill his will.
>
> On December 8, 1991, my wife and I were baptized, and in February our daughter was baptized. Finally we had found happiness; our lives had changed; the goal and desire was revealed to us to follow the single, true path which the Savior has shown us.

Slava was to play a major leadership role in the Church in Kiev. First a branch president, Slava Gulko became president of the new Left Bank District in February 1993, which oversees all of the branches in that region of Kiev. The hope of Slava's Jewish grandfather, seventy years ago, that his descendant would be a spiritual leader to the people of Kiev had been fulfilled.

Slava, Zoya, and Kira Gulko were sealed for eternity in the Freiberg Germany Temple in 1993 when they led the travel group of Saints to the temple. They also led several other travel groups of Latter-day Saints to the Freiberg temple during 1993 and 1994.

Zoya Translates the Book of Mormon

Zoya Gulko was baptized at the time we were searching for a member of the Church who would have the unusual skills necessary to translate the Book of Mormon into the Ukrainian language. At that time, that book of scripture was available only in Russian.

Elder Steven Struk, director of the translation project in Kiev, and I were praying that one possessing such gifts would come into the Church, because we had learned that non-members would not be considered by the Translation Department in Salt Lake City.

Zoya was baptized just at this time. She was interviewed and tested and found to be a truly outstanding candidate for this assignment.

The translation of the Book of Mormon into a new language normally takes a number of years to complete. Zoya was blessed with an unusual spiritual gift to complete the initial manuscript of the Ukrainian translation in nineteen months, an unbelievable feat considering that she was required also to continue her full-time job as a teacher of English at the special school to financially support her family during the difficult period of economic hyperinflation. She also served as a district Young Women president in Kiev.

Zoya has related sacred experiences that came to her during the process of translation late into the night. She experienced the power of revelation and the gift of tongues in which words came to her in a spiritual stream, beyond her previous understanding and ability. Her testimony of the Book of Mormon as a holy scripture of God has become profoundly strong.

It is interesting to observe that in a society in which Jews have had a tragic history, the Lord chose a son and a daughter of Judah to help lay the foundations of the Church of Jesus Christ and provide his marvelous spiritual blessings for the people of Ukraine.

Leonid Finds "Something Beautiful"

The search of Leonid, who as the son of leading figures in the Ukrainian Academy of Sciences sought for an alternative path to the atheism of his upbringing, was also discussed in chapter two. His search had taken him through Eastern medicine, philosophies, and religions. In his search he says that he felt "an expectation of something beautiful" that would happen in his life.

One Sunday morning Leonid was strolling with his children when Elders John Lunt and Richard Davis, assistants to the mission president, were walking swiftly past him on their way to a meeting. Leonid describes what happened next: "Suddenly one of them turned back and came up to us. We talked to these young men. I will always thank God for this first fleeting meeting on the street with these beautiful men. They were in a hurry, but felt impressed to stop.

"They opened up to me the world of the Bible and the Book of Mormon. They helped me find faith, answered my questions, brought to me that beautiful something for which I had been searching and waiting."

Brother Leonid became an outstanding Gospel Doctrine teacher in Kiev. Then he served as a branch president. He was among the group of leaders chosen to go to Salt Lake City to complete the preparation of the Ukrainian translation tape for temple ordinances in November 1994. In the temple in Salt Lake City, he found the pinnacle of spiritual experience for which he had hungered all his life.

Sergei's Search for Modern Prophets

Sergei is a senior engineer in a major state enterprise in Kiev. As recounted earlier, he had often meditated about the Bible, asking himself and others: "If the Bible is true, why are there no prophets today? Why are there no miracles and revelations in our time? Has God's attitude changed toward us?" No one could give him satisfactory answers to these questions.

President Biddulph greets district missionary Elder Koshkarev before his departure to a full-time mission in Russia.

One day Sergei met two young Latter-day Saint missionaries on the street. They asked him about his beliefs concerning religion, and he repeated the questions that had concerned him for many years.

The missionaries assured him that God is the same today as he was in ancient times and that there are prophets, revelation, and miracles in our day. As evidence for their claim, they introduced him to the Book of Mormon. Sergei made an appointment with them for his family to hear more in their apartment and to receive a copy of the Book of Mormon.

After telling his wife about the appointment, Sergei had second thoughts about meeting with the elders. The word *Mormon* seemed like a very "foreign and frightful word," a feeling of "something dangerous," as he describes it. They looked up this strange word in an encyclopedia and read the very negative Communist presentation of Mormons and polygamy. At first they decided to cancel the appointment, but as they continued to think about it, a feeling of comfort came over them, assuring them that all would be well.

Sergei has written about meeting with the missionaries: "Our meetings became regular. We learned about The Church of Jesus Christ of Latter-day Saints, about Joseph Smith, the Prophet, about the Book of Mormon. We learned about the plan of salvation of our Lord Jesus Christ and other important information. At that time I made a choice. I came to believe in God and in his Son Jesus Christ, and his great sacrifice for me."

Together with his wife and children, Sergei read the Book of Mormon:

> I received a testimony that the Book of Mormon is true through the witness of the Holy Ghost, which feeling is described by the Apostle Paul in Galatians 5:22: "But the fruit of the Spirit is love, joy, peace." I felt that love, joy, peace as I read and prayed about the Book of Mormon. I accepted the Book of Mormon as scripture very quickly.
>
> As I read and studied, I understood that our Heavenly Father had forgiven my sins through the sacrifice of his Only Begotten Son, Jesus Christ. He accepted my repentance. He chose me and led me to the true church. Thanks to God, I have the full restored gospel. I know that my Heavenly Father loves me and blesses my family. At first I only believed that. Now I am sure that it is true. This assurance has changed my entire life.
>
> Our family was baptized on the 4th of July, 1993. I am happy that my wife and my children believe in God with me. I know that this is also a blessing of our Heavenly Father. Our life became joyful and full of peace, spiritual and purposeful. I see how much we have changed.

Sergei was called as an elders quorum president in Kiev, and he later became branch president and then a counselor in the district presidency. Sergei Mutilin and his entire family were sealed together for eternity in the Freiberg Germany Temple in 1994.

Dmitry the Believer Finds a Book

A few days before Elders Richard Davis, Thomas Wright, Brandon Arrington, and Jesus Condori arrived to open a new city, an unusual event occurred. A professor at the state university named Dmitry discovered a strange book in a bookstore entitled *Kniga mormona* (the Book of Mormon in Russian).

Elder Ray Sheffield (top row, third from right) and Sister Annette Sheffield (center of second row) assist leaders and members of new Lesnoy branch in Kiev, 1993.

A Russian born in Siberia, Dmitry was converted to Christianity while serving in the Soviet Red Army, where he read the New Testament. After completing military service, he attended the Russian Orthodox Seminary, where he was a brilliant student. Dmitry was unable to accept some of the doctrines and practices of the Russian Orthodox Church, so he was not ordained. As an unordained religious activist, he was arrested and spent three years in terrible prison camps.

After his release, Dmitry found opportunity during the more liberal Gorbachev era to teach a course at the university titled "The Bible As Literature," which was in actuality a course on biblical theology and religious philosophy. Since he was both a brilliant teacher and a believer, the principal churches in that area sent priests and ministers to be trained by him, in the absence of a theological seminary.

Then came the day in May when Dmitry discovered the Russian copy of the Book of Mormon in a local bookstore. Its impact upon him was somewhat like the experience of Parley P. Pratt. Dmitry read the book nonstop, and when he finished, he felt a deep conviction that he had indeed discovered "another testament of Jesus Christ."

A few days later he met Elder Wright and Elder Condori on the street, almost immediately after their arrival in the large city.

Dmitry suffered persecution for his conversion to the restored gospel. He was banned from teaching priests of the Russian Orthodox Church and also banned from entering any of its church buildings or facilities. The Orthodox bishop attempted to get the university rector to fire Dmitry because he had become a Latter-day Saint. Twice he was attacked by young thugs on the street, who beat him into unconsciousness and took his belongings.

Dmitry became the first branch president of the Church in his city and remains a devoted spiritual leader and teacher in the Church. Although living in great poverty, he is positive, loving, and full of faith in God.

Pyotr Finds the Latter-Day Church

Pyotr, the self-proclaimed "Mormon" physician in Minsk, Belarus, was discussed in chapter two. Pyotr's father had been taught the gospel and baptized a Latter-day Saint by an American serviceman in Western Europe during World War II. He taught his son, Pyotr, about Mormonism from a small notebook he brought back with him. All of his life, Pyotr had hungered to read the Book of Mormon and join the Church. Although he attended the Baptist Church in Minsk, Pyotr told everyone who knew him that he was a Mormon.

The advertising of Elder Russell M. Nelson's visit and of his public address in Minsk brought Pyotr into contact with visiting representatives of the Church. His first contacts and teachers were Elders James Udy and Newell Anthony Brown, who gave him his first copy of the Book of Mormon. A short time later, two humanitarian volunteers from America, Elders Daniel P. Reneau and D. Chalk Simons, taught Pyotr.

Elder Reneau remembers that Pyotr had an unusual understanding of the gospel, like that of a lifelong member of the Church. "He taught us the discussions more than we taught him. He studied the Book of Mormon constantly and had a deep understanding of it. He had read the Book of Mormon entirely four times before his baptism." Elder Reneau believes that Pyotr's broad understanding of the gospel could have come to him only through his father's oral teaching, for he possessed no Church literature before meeting the elders.

Pyotr is a faithful, enthusiastic member of the Minsk Central Branch. The Lord has answered his lifelong prayer that he could receive the gospel, read the Book of Mormon, and be baptized a Latter-day Saint. In gratitude to the Lord for this blessing, Pyotr continues to publicly proclaim the gospel and to do everything possible to serve and to minister to others in the Church. This forty-year-old physician has found, at last, the precious "pearl of great price."

Chapter 8

"I WAS LED BY THE SPIRIT"

"And I was led by the Spirit, not knowing beforehand the things which I should do."
—1 Nephi 4:6

The time-honored method of going from door to door, seeking contacts to teach, was not used in Ukraine and Belarus during the years of our mission. In the beginning we deemed door-to-door "tracting" too invasive of privacy and foreign to the traditions of the country. We knew the Lord had prepared many choice souls to receive the gospel, people whom he would lead to us if we were visible in public places where people talk as they wait to be served and if we were outgoing, friendly, and fearless in following the promptings of his Spirit.

Referrals from members and current investigators were normally a very productive means of finding good contacts, so missionaries were encouraged to use that method. Some converts found the Church through hearing of its meetings and deciding to attend. The predominant means of locating new religious seekers, however, was street contacting using the model of 1 Nephi 4:6: "And I was led by the Spirit, not knowing beforehand the things which I should do."

Whenever they were not teaching investigators, working with members, or serving in other vital and meaningful ways, missionaries were expected to go out to public places where people gathered, such as a marketplace, a bus stop, or on the crowded tram or metro. At such times they were to let the Spirit guide them as they conversed with people in a friendly,

Missionary couples with special assignments. Seated: Sister Jean Struk and Elder Steven Struk (Ukrainian translation program). Standing, left to right: Elder Alexander Bigney (office administration) and Sister Rose Bigney (mission medical advisor); President and Sister Biddulph; Sister Shirley Porath and Elder Preston Porath (physical facilities program); Sister Shirley Moffett and Elder Max Moffett (Church Educational System).

nonaggressive manner. Over and over we proved the truth of the Lord's promise: "Yea, open your mouths and spare not, and you shall be laden with sheaves upon your backs, for lo, I am with you" (D&C 33:9).

Misha's Miracle

One day at a public square, Elder Cody Hill and Elder Daniel Reneau met a man who invited them to come to his home for a religious discussion. He said his name was Misha (a nickname for Mikhail) and gave them his telephone number rather than address, asking them to call before coming. The telephone number he gave to them turned out to be that of someone else whose name was also Misha (Mikhail). This second Misha had been earnestly praying for spiritual guidance. He has written an account of his conversion experience:

> In April 1993, we received a phone call in our apartment. I picked up the phone and a young man with a

foreign accent began speaking. He said that he was from America, from the Mormon Church, and wanted to arrange a meeting to talk about God. He also said that we had met on a square which is near our home, and that I had given my telephone number to him.

I was very surprised because, actually, I had never met him and have never given out my telephone number to a stranger. Nevertheless, I invited him to come to our home the following evening, for I was seeking religious truth. [The phone call was on Sunday, April 25, 1993].

On Monday at the appointed time, two polite young men in white shirts and ties (Elder Hill and Elder Reneau) came to our home. The elders had recently met a young couple in our area, and we were all surprised to find that the husband, whose name was Misha, had given them his telephone number which turned out to be ours. Then I remembered that I had earnestly prayed and asked God to help me in my spiritual condition, which was very difficult. Could this be a miraculous answer to my prayer?

The elders talked with us and opened our understanding to many new truths about God and Jesus Christ. We found out about the Book of Mormon. My wife, Lena, before this time did not believe in God, just as I had once not believed. Thanks to these truths and the presence of the Holy Ghost (that I know for sure now), my wife gradually gained faith in our Father in Heaven. We were also greatly impressed by the spiritual character of the elders. On May 16, 1993, I, my wife Lena, and my older daughter Nastia were baptized. (My younger daughter wanted very badly to be baptized, but was only five years old.) That day will forever be remembered. We are so grateful to the Lord for answering my prayers and for bringing us into His Church.

Misha is now a Church leader in his city. He and his wife and their two children have since traveled to Freiberg, Germany, to receive their eternal temple blessings as a family.

Found Twice by the Spirit

Elder Matt Ericson and his companion were fasting and praying that they might be able to fulfill an assignment from their mission president to find and baptize a man suited to be the president of a new branch that would soon be formed in their area. One day they met Sergei for the first time at a bus stop. Returning from a long camping trip, Sergei was unshaven, dirty, and dressed in old clothing. His physical appearance might have deterred the missionaries from making his acquaintance, but Elder Ericson felt a strong impression to approach him and to discuss the restored gospel. Sergei gave the elders his address and invited them to visit him the next day.

Later the elders realized that the address Sergei had given them was incomplete. Unable to locate him, they reluctantly went on with their other work. Sergei waited in vain for the elders to come. He was disappointed that they had missed the appointment. When he realized that he may have given them an incorrect or incomplete address, Sergei felt a strange urgency to search for the two strangers. It seemed unlikely that in a city of several million people he could find them again, but he spent several hours trying.

Several days later the missionaries passed the same bus stop again and were frantically hailed by a well-groomed, impressive looking man who appeared to know them. He introduced himself as Sergei, the man with whom they had made the previous appointment. Given Sergei's recent haircut and shave and the fact that he was suitably dressed for his profession as an executive, the missionaries never would have recognized him.

The missionaries met with Sergei, his wife, Valya, who is a professional teacher and linguist, and their children. Soon all were baptized. Two months later Sergei was called to preside over a branch being organized in that part of the city. Valya became an outstanding seminary teacher and translator of curriculum materials for the Church.

Sergei felt a persistent impression to invite his brother, Alexei, along with Alexei's wife and children, to visit him and hear the gospel. Sergei delayed acting on the impression because he was sure Alexei had no interest in religion and also because he lived a great distance away. When Sergei did invite the family for a visit, great blessings resulted: the family accepted the gospel, were all baptized, and became the first Latter-day Saints in their entire area of the country.

Upon being introduced to Alexei, the impression came to me that he, like Sergei, would one day become a fine Church leader. When the city where Sergei's family live was finally opened, Alexei was called to be president of the first branch of the Church organized there. Both brothers and their families have since received their eternal temple blessings.

Elder Ericson and Sergei have often expressed their gratitude to the Lord for bringing them together, not once, but twice, so that an extended, elect family could accept the gospel of Jesus Christ and the Church in Ukraine could receive strong leadership for two cities.

Finding the Wrong Volodya

Elders Richard Davis and Richard Jackson were street contacting one day when they met a man who called himself Volodya. This man invited them to his apartment, gave them an address, and set a date and time to meet them.

Arriving at the apartment, the elders met a woman who they expected was Volodya's wife and told her that he had made an appointment with them. She invited them in, and they waited for Volodya. After a few minutes a neighboring family also joined them.

Then a strange thing happened. When the husband returned, it was evident that he was not the Volodya who had invited them, although his name also was Volodya. Nevertheless, the two families invited them to stay and teach the first missionary discussion. Both families were spiritual seekers and were ultimately baptized. The wrong address turned out to be the right place to find the elect.

The Lord Sends Comfort

Another Volodya lived in a different major Ukrainian city. He was a man of considerable responsibility in his profession,

Voskresenka Branch Relief Society has a special activity.

but his world had just collapsed. Volodya had been through the trying experience of watching his beloved wife die of cancer. At the time of her death, he had had no religion in his life. He was devastated, dazed, and confused.

Shortly after his wife's passing, Volodya was walking and sadly pondering what had happened to him when he met two young men, obviously foreigners from America, on a park path. These two young men were Elder Russell van der Werf and his companion, Elder Scott Flake.

The elders warmly greeted Volodya, and then Elder van der Werf was led by the Spirit of discernment to boldly say to him: "The Lord has sent us to find you today, to bring you a message of comfort, peace, and joy."

Volodya was touched to the core of his being and agreed to a gospel discussion on the spot. At the close of this discussion, Elder van der Werf committed him to be baptized. Volodya agreed to be baptized if he could receive the spiritual confirmation that the elders had promised him. After brief reflection, he realized that he had already received a powerful witness of the Spirit as these splendid young men boldly testified to him. He knew they were servants of God sent to help him in this dark night of his soul. He quickly accepted their invitation to baptism.

Within a few months, Volodya was the president of a new branch of the Church. In the process of serving others,

Volodya has found the peace and joy that the elders had promised him.

Tatyana Feels the Spirit

Tatyana has described her first meeting with two sister missionaries: "My first missionaries were Sister Melanie Gamble and Sister Angela Cicerone. I can say precisely that I came to the Church because of their eyes. As we met on the street, I beheld in their eyes the greatness of God's love for me. They had a piece of that divine love, and they gave it as a present to me."

Tatyana could not deny the marvelous presence of the Holy Spirit that was with her as she met with the sisters. "It was not the logic of the arguments of the missionaries that affected me, not the plausibility of Joseph Smith's story, but the evident great power of their faith which permeated every word they spoke, even the shining look on their faces. The total faith of their very being testified to me that their message was true. I felt a heavenly love radiating from them to God and to me."

Life had not been easy for Tatyana, but she felt the assurance that God had led the sister missionaries to her. After her baptism, Tatyana served many others with the same love she discerned in the missionaries.

Tamara Finds Her Redeemer

Tamara is a grandmother who, like many others in the older generation, has experienced almost indescribable suffering in her life. At a moment of great despair, the Lord brought her the gift of his wonderful gospel as two missionaries were led by the Spirit to contact her in the Kiev metro. I will let her tell the story:

> I always felt all alone in the world, although I had relatives, friends, and family. I turned my thoughts to God in many times of want and despair. It seemed to me that the forces of evil were all around me. I worried about my

daughter, granddaughter, mother, sisters, and brothers. Their suffering tormented me.

I prayed, asking God to save my family, my relatives, and friends. There were many serious problems: economic, medical, and spiritual. Then came that wonderful day when I met the missionaries in the metro [subway]. There I met my dear Elder [Brian] Jarman and Elder [Benjamin] Lutes. I invited them to my home.

Their visit was like a beam of light in the darkness. It was the light of the gospel. I tried very hard to understand what my Heavenly Father was telling me through these dear servants of God. I learned for the first time that I have a Redeemer, a Savior—Jesus Christ.

My dear teachers described to me how our Savior suffered, how he redeemed the sins of us all. I wept as I contemplated his sufferings. The sufferings of my life seemed no longer significant in comparison with the sufferings of our Savior for me. I rejoiced in his love for me and that he knows what I have gone through in my life.

The missionaries helped me find God, our Heavenly Father, in prayer. Now I feel him and his Only Begotten Son always near me. I know he answers my prayers for my family, my friends, and my missionaries who baptized me and my granddaughter on September 5, 1992.

I obtained hope and joy—the hope to be with my Heavenly Father forever. I try to keep all his commandments. Every day I pray for him to give me wisdom, patience, and love. He has blessed me greatly—temporally and spiritually. I ask him to give me the strength to endure to the end.

A Family's Simultaneous Conversion in Two Cities

One day in a city of our mission an inebriated man at a bus stop wanted to talk with Elder Anthony Brown. This often happened when drunken men and women saw young elders and sisters, and it was rarely productive, so Elder Brown tried to avoid the man. Still the man persisted, and something prompted Elder Brown to talk with him.

Reluctantly Elder Brown made an appointment to meet

Some of the sisters rendering compassionate service in the Kiev Central Branch, spring 1994.

the man and his family at their apartment. When the elders arrived, this person was drunk again, but he introduced his family and his wife's sister, who was visiting from Riga, Latvia.

The man was not interested in hearing the gospel, but his wife and family and the visiting aunt quickly accepted the teachings of the Church. Then the aunt explained that she had returned to the city to divorce her husband, who remained in Riga, because of the physical abuse she was suffering from his problem with alcohol.

Her acceptance of the gospel made her reconsider her decision to obtain a divorce. She called her husband in Riga and told him of her desire to be baptized into the LDS Church, and of her desire to return and try to work out the problems of their marriage.

Her husband astounded her by relating that he had met the Mormon elders on the street in Riga after her departure. He had believed their message and read the Book of Mormon. And most astounding of all, he had not had a drink since the start of his discussions with the missionaries in Riga. He had been praying that the Lord would soften her heart to forgive him. She did.

The Lord miraculously reunited this couple by bringing each of them to the missionaries, each simultaneously in separate cities. This couple was baptized together and began a new life of reconciliation.

Red Army Officer Finds the Gospel

Vasily was the Soviet military officer in the general staff in Moscow who bravely defied the orders of the junta during the attempted coup in August 1991 (see chapter five). Vasily was born in 1956 of mixed Russian and Ukrainian peasant parentage in Kazakhstan during the time of Nikita Khrushchev's campaign to open up a new agricultural zone in the virgin lands of that republic. His parents were part of the "Virgin Lands Campaign," which was an attempt to open a whole new agricultural region. His parents were agricultural workers, but they moved back to Ukraine in 1957, where their son grew to manhood and finished high school in the little village of Piryatin.

Vasily was a model member of the Komsomol (the Young Communist League), which was the youth auxiliary of the Communist Party. He was admitted to the Kiev Military Academy in 1973, graduating in 1978. This was an officer training school for the Soviet Red Army. In 1978 he also was admitted to the Communist Party. This was considered an honor as well as a necessary "entrance ticket" to the leadership echelon of the military, as well as to other professions in the Soviet Union.

Vasily married, and two daughters were born to him and his wife, Lidia, in the years that followed: Tatyana in 1977 and Darya in 1979. Lidia graduated from the Kiev Pedagogical Institute of Foreign Languages and was especially accomplished in the English language. Vasily attained a high rank as a military officer and was a specialist in communications in the command center in Moscow at the time of the attempted political coup.

Although he was a member of the Communist Party, Vasily, as well as Lidia, began to feel the same spiritual vacuum that many others were feeling during the 1980s. Vasily explains: "All my life in the totalitarian system has prepared me and my family to accept the gospel. I tried to find out the truth, although I was sure that the USSR was the best country in the world. In 1986–1987, I began to think about God, and I bought a New Testament. I read it, but I could not understand it well. Nevertheless, I understood that it was impossible to do a righteous deed without feeling God's love."

After the coup had failed and the independence of Ukraine had been proclaimed, Vasily and his family returned to Kiev for posting by the new Ukrainian Armed Forces. Vasily and Lidia had already received a letter from Tanya, a friend in Kiev, in which she described her conversion to The Church of Jesus Christ of Latter-day Saints.

Vasily writes: "We remembered a negative hero in one of Conan Doyle's novels, who was a Mormon. The choice of churches of our friend Tanya seemed strange to us."

When Vasily and Lidia and their family returned to Kiev, Tanya invited them to attend church with her. Vasily describes this experience: "When we visited this first meeting, I felt a strong conviction at once that the restored gospel is true. . . . I was surprised to see the open, beautiful faces of the people there. We got acquainted with the missionaries, whose names were Elder (Brian) Jarman and Elder [Benjamin] Lutes. We had two discussions with them. They gave us the Book of Mormon. . . . My wife and I understood that accepting this gospel would be the only way to save our children."

Vasily was assigned to be a commander in the Odessa military district, far from the closest branch of the Church and the missionaries. Vasily writes: "We read and accepted the Book of Mormon and prayed to our Heavenly Father with only one request—that we could have a military assignment in Kiev where we could be taught and could attend church. One week later this prayer was answered, as I was suddenly transferred to the general staff of the military forces of Ukraine in Kiev in the Ministry of Defense."

On November 13 they returned to Kiev and attended the

LDS Church. Sister Merinda Hill and Sister Georgianna Standiford completed teaching the gospel discussions to this family, and on 3 January 1993, all four members were baptized.

Vasily was called to be a branch president within a few months. His Young Men and Young Women programs were particularly outstanding, a model for the whole mission. He was then called to major leadership responsibilities at the district and mission levels.

Lidia has served as a youth and women's leader and as a member of the Ukrainian language translation project in Kiev. The children, Tanya and Darya, have been youth leaders.

On 26 April 1994, all four members of Vasily and Lidia's family were sealed in the Freiberg Germany Temple. Vasily organized and led this temple trip, as well as several succeeding temple trips. In September 1994, a third little girl was born under the temple covenant to Vasily and Lidia. After fasting and prayer, Vasily retired from his position in the Ukraine military so that he would be more available to serve the Lord. He was among the leadership group chosen to go to the Salt Lake Temple in November 1994 to help prepare the Ukrainian translation tape for temple ordinances.

Vasily closes his written account of his conversion with these words:

> Before my baptism, I thought that the strongest one is always right. I am physically strong, and I had a high position in the Army. I thought that I could stand up for myself. I loved to defend my subordinates from the anger of the head. . . .
>
> The gospel has already changed and constantly changes and improves my life. Moreover, I know that it will be so forever. I must only endure to the end. I pray to my Heavenly Father that he will help me on this way back to him. He always helps me. I have had many life situations when our Heavenly Father helped me specifically. He showed me the way—the right way—after prayer. Through fasting and prayer I have seen seriously ill patients recover

and be healed, through the anointing of the priesthood. All my life I have tried to honestly serve my people. Every day I read the scriptures. Through daily prayer and daily scripture study I receive personal inspiration and answers for the decisions I must make in my life.

These are a few of the many experiences I have recorded that show how the Holy Spirit connects those seekers who are ready with the missionaries who are spiritually prepared to teach them the gospel of Jesus Christ. The Lord is the Good Shepherd who knows and gathers his sheep. The scriptures tell us: "And he gathereth his children from the four quarters of the earth; and he numbereth his sheep, and they know him; and there shall be one fold and one shepherd; and he shall feed his sheep, and in him they shall find pasture" (1 Nephi 22:25).

What a beautiful pasture it is.

Chapter 9

"MINE ANGELS SHALL GO UP BEFORE YOU"

"But I say unto you: Mine angels shall go up
before you, and also my presence, and in time
ye shall possess the goodly land"

—D&C 103:19–20

Proclaiming the gospel is a divine call to labor in a vineyard with the Lord and his angels, who are already working there even before the coming of the first missionaries. The Lord has promised us through a modern prophet:

"Therefore, let not your hearts faint, for I say not unto you as I said unto your fathers: Mine angel shall go up before you, but not my presence.

"But I say unto you: Mine angels shall go up before you, and also my presence, and in time ye shall possess the goodly land" (D&C 103:19–20).

Just as Amulek in Ammonihah was prepared by an angel for the coming of Alma (see Alma 8:16–20; 10:7–10), the Lord in our day often sends his spiritual emissaries beforehand to prepare the way before the coming of his earthly emissaries. This was clearly evident through sacred experiences reported by Latter-day Saints in each of the nine cities we opened for proselyting in Ukraine and Belarus. The Lord was already there ahead of us, preparing the way and specific people for our coming, as the following accounts demonstrate.

Vera's Dream

Vera was one of the early converts in Kiev. Since the time she was a young girl, Vera periodically had a special dream. In the dream she was promised that the true way to God would one day be shown to her and that it would bring her great happiness. At times of great tribulation for her, the dream would come again, assuring her of the Lord's love and the future blessings she would receive if her faith remained strong.

As a young girl during World War II, Vera was separated from her family and held in a work camp in Germany. After the war she was reunited with her mother in Ukraine. In very destitute conditions, Vera nursed her beloved mother until a lingering, painful death of this loved one left Vera alone again.

Vera married, and a daughter was born. Then she cared for her husband in his illness and watched him die, leaving her alone again, this time with a young child to care for. As she grew old, Vera also suffered serious health problems that took her to the brink of death. Yet she was always comforted by the recurring dream that promised a future way of happiness.

Shortly before a very serious operation, in which her life hung in the balance, this aged widow again had her special dream. She was assured that she would survive the operation and be restored to health. Shown the beautiful faces of two fair-haired young men who would soon teach her the true path to God, Vera was promised great happiness and peace if she would accept their message. These were unique, unforgettable faces she saw, unlike any young men she had ever seen in Kiev or Ukraine. She assumed they would be foreigners.

After her recovery, Vera was shopping in downtown Kiev when she recognized with unspeakable joy the faces of two young men dressed in suits and ties—the very faces she had seen in her dream! Like aged Anna in the temple at Jerusalem (see Luke 2:36–38), she had waited throughout her life for the messengers of God.

Members of the Church in Minsk, Belarus, 1993, six months after beginning the work there.

Elders Aaron Love and Rory Allen were assigned to the area of Kiev where Vera lived, and their own apartment was very close to Vera's home. As a result of meeting them, she received the gospel with joy and was baptized.

In spite of her age, Vera has become a great gospel scholar and a teacher of the Book of Mormon and the Bible. One of my choicest experiences was to attend an Easter Sunday service in her branch and to hear her give one of the truly great sermons I have heard in my lifetime on the Savior Jesus Christ, his suffering and death, his atonement for sin, and his great resurrection. On that sacred occasion, Vera blended movingly the testimonies of Matthew, Mark, Luke, John, and Nephi, as well as her own gentle, loving witness of these events.

Vera lived and saved her widow's mite for the time when she could travel with other members of the Church to the temple of God in Freiberg, Germany, to receive her ordinances and to be sealed to her husband and deceased family. Many years before, she had been sent to that area of Germany as a fearful young girl by the German troops that had occupied her country in World War II. Now, with joy, Vera returned to the same area where she had received her first dream of the gospel, this time to partake of all the ordinances of eternal life. She had lived true to her name: Vera, "the woman of faith."

Alla's Dream

Alla lived in the city of Donetsk. She had a dream in which she saw a bridge over a deep chasm. A young man beckoned her to follow him across the bridge to a beautiful land on the other side, where she would reside in the presence of God. She could never forget this sacred dream that was unlike any dream she had ever experienced, nor could she forget the very singular, "non-Slavic face" she beheld.

In late 1992, shortly after this dream, Alla was invited by a friend to attend one of the early meetings of The Church of Jesus Christ of Latter-day Saints in the central library of Donetsk. When she arrived at the meeting, she was greeted at the door by Elder James Harris, whose face she had seen in the dream. Alla did not tell him about this experience until after she had been baptized.

Anna's Premonition

Anna lives in the Borshchagovka District of Kiev with her husband, Anatoly, and daughter, Yulia. One night she had a dream in which she saw two beautiful, but unusual, faces of young men. The next day she was shocked to see two young men in suits at the nearby market who had the unusual faces she had seen in the dream.

What can it mean? she asked herself. She talked with these young men and found out that they were Mormon missionaries. She wanted to invite them to her home but hesitated because of what her husband might think of her. How could she explain her interest in two young, attractive, foreign men? Reluctantly she walked away.

The next day Anatoly told her he had invited two young missionaries for dinner and a gospel discussion. *Can it be the same young men she had seen in the market?* Anna asked herself. When Elder Aaron Love and Elder Rory Allen arrived, she beheld with joy and amazement that they were indeed the

Elders Ryan Gibby, Gordon Roylance (baptizing), and Curtis Bingham at the baptism of a family in the Black Sea at Odessa.

faces in her dream, the same two young men she had met in the market.

Anna, Anatoly, and Yulia quickly accepted the message of the restored gospel and were soon baptized. Anna became the branch Relief Society president and was later called to be the district Relief Society president, serving with great love, compassion, and skill. Anatoly soon was called as a counselor to the branch president. Then, when a new branch was created, Anatoly was called as branch president. Yulia is a fine piano student at the Kiev Conservatory of Music and serves in many music responsibilities in the branch and district. She has also accepted the call as district Young Single Adult representative.

Anna, Anatoly, and Yulia invited Colleen and me to a farewell dinner at their apartment a few days before our departure from the mission. They spent the evening speaking to us of the joy they had found in the gospel and in the temple, of their gratitude to the Lord and to the missionaries who prepared them for baptism nearly three years before. They continue to bear witness that the Lord prepared them for his emissaries in the unusual dream that Anna experienced.

Angels Prepare the Harvest

In each of the nine cities that we opened in Ukraine and Belarus, we saw indications that the Lord's spiritual emissaries had already been there before us, preparing specific people for the coming of the missionaries. For example, as related earlier, the four missionaries who opened Kharkov baptized in their first few weeks a number of converts who had considerable leadership abilities. I took occasion during my first monthly visit to Kharkov to interview a number of these wonderful new converts. I was amazed and humbled to hear so many of them tell me sacred experiences—events that had helped prepare them to recognize and receive the restored gospel—that had happened to them just before the arrival of the missionaries.

The same was true for members in other cities we visited. In Odessa, as in Kharkov, a large number of choice people, many of whom would be future leaders, were baptized during the first two months. Again, as I interviewed new converts, they volunteered to share the same kind of sacred personal experiences as those discussed above. Similarly remarkable spiritual experiences occurred in Minsk. The pattern of events became so predictable that as each set of missionaries was sent to open a new city, I felt I could promise them that angels were already there. I encouraged them to live close to the Spirit so that the Lord could bring to them those whom he had prepared.

When the Lord's servants are clean, seek to know his will, and learn to recognize and obey his promptings, fearing not to act as he has inspired them to act, he is able to work great miracles through their efforts.

From what I have seen, I am certain that the Lord makes the same promise to missionaries opening new cities in our day that he made to the Apostle Paul and later to the Prophet Joseph Smith: "For I am with thee, and no man shall set on thee to hurt thee: for I have much people in this city" (Acts 18:10; see also D&C 111:2–11).

Chapter 10

SONS AND DAUGHTERS
OF A KING

Called to know the richness of his blessing—
Sons and daughters, children of a King—
Glad of heart, his holy name confessing,
Praises unto him we bring.
　　　　　—"Called to Serve," *Hymns,* no. 249

God of wisdom, God of truth,
Take us in our eager youth;
Lift us step by step to thee
Thru an endless ministry.
　　　　　—"God of Power, God of Right," *Hymns,* no. 20

Oksana is single and in her mid-twenties. While completing her diploma at a pedagogical university, she is also working as a teacher of children in the early primary grades.

Of her early religious training from her grandmother, Oksana writes: "When I was five years old, my grandmother told me about God and the Bible. I often heard her prayers before and after meals and before sleeping. She even taught me how to pray, but I was a small child and did not understand anything. From that time I wondered why my grandmother loved God and Jesus Christ so much. Why did she pray? I did not receive the answers to these questions for fifteen years."

Oksana grew up very unhappy, with a keen sense of injustice in the world. "It was hard for me to live. There was hate, misunderstanding, envy, and cruelness around me, but something told me inside my mind that there was comfort and happiness somewhere. Where? I became sad and offensive toward others. Nothing brought joy to me. I did not see any justice in life. Honest people lived badly, but bad people seemed to prosper. I could not understand why it was so. These kinds of feelings tortured me for five years."

One day in early February 1991, the elementary school where Oksana taught invited some LDS missionaries to visit the school and speak English with the children and tell them about their home countries of the United States and Australia. As the missionaries spoke to the children in her class, Oksana "got a warm feeling towards them at once," she recalls. "And when they began to speak, I understood and felt how much they loved people and how they wanted to help them. I listened carefully to everything they had to say."

Oksana desired to continue these discussions with the missionaries after school. "For the first time in my life, I came to feel that we need to believe in the living God. The Orthodox Church was not attractive to me, . . . but there were young, beautiful people here. They showed me how to love and trust God, that he loves and takes care of us."

She accepted invitations from the missionaries to attend church and to study the gospel. As she received the message of the restored gospel, her outlook brightened and life took on new meaning for her. She explains:

> The missionaries had profound and beautiful answers to all of the questions that I had about life. I took hope in their assurance that God's justice and mercy will, in the end, prevail over evil.
>
> At first when I read the Book of Mormon, I understood almost nothing. Then I prayed, as I had been advised in the beginning. Nothing strange or spectacular happened to me, but I became more peaceful and patient. Peace grew in my heart, and I gradually began to understand what I was reading and to look at the same things in a new way. The restoration of the gospel came into my mind, heart, and

Three Latter-day Saint young adults relax from their university studies, 1994.

soul. Sincerity and hope returned to me. I stopped being sad and pessimistic. These changes brought me to baptism.

The missionaries did not have to work a lot with me. I obtained an understanding of many things during our discussions. I did not search for any other churches before my baptism. Our Church is the first that brought me to the gospel, and I joyfully accepted it. My baptism day was the happiest day of my entire life. The gift of the Holy Ghost is my peace and my joy in a dreary world.

I am happy that God allowed me to be a member of the true Church. The gospel has significantly changed my life. I have had the great joy of attending the holy temple two times, to receive my own endowment, and to perform baptisms and endowments for the dead. To attend the temple is a glorious homecoming visit to my Eternal Father and my kindred dead."

From Orphan to Servant of God

Aleksei was born in a small town in southern Ukraine. His mother passed away when he was a child, and his father died while Aleksei was a student, leaving him an orphan. He and his only sister have a great love and closeness for each other. Aleksei has poor eyesight and received the opportunity to receive his secondary education and advanced postsecondary education in special schools for those with visual impairment.

One day Elder Quinton Spencer and Elder Brian Higbee were invited to address Aleksei's class at his postsecondary institute. They told about their mission and about the calling of Joseph Smith, and they introduced the Book of Mormon.

Aleksei found them interesting but was not at all impressed to investigate Mormonism. He grudgingly accepted one of their business cards with their telephone number, but threw it into his bag with the thought: *I'll never need this. I'm definitely not interested.*

As he walked along the street after class, a powerful impression came to Aleksei: *The missionaries have spoken the word of the Lord to you. Their message is true. The Book of Mormon is true. You are to become a Mormon.* He was greatly surprised at this thought but felt certain it had come from God.

"From that moment I totally changed my thinking," Aleksei recalls. "I knew that Mormonism was true and that I would, indeed, become a Latter-day Saint. The more I thought about it, the more enthusiastic I felt. By the time I got home, I was excited at the prospect."

Aleksei immediately called the elders. He considered himself all ready to be baptized but was afraid that the elders would not agree, so he asked only to see them and study further. He began to meet with them regularly.

Aleksei's sister had recently become an Adventist and was not happy with his choice of the LDS Church. She tried to persuade him to reconsider his decision. He attended Adventist meetings, lectures, and read the literature of this group, but he felt reinforced in his decision to join The Church of Jesus Christ of Latter-day Saints.

"My baptism was the most wonderful day of my life and the beginning of great spiritual progress," he says.

Aleksei became not only a diligent student of the scriptures but also soon became known as an outstanding teacher

Ukrainian Sister Olesya Vershigora, serving at Temple Square in Salt Lake City, greets Ruth Biddulph, 1994.

of youth in his branch. Although only three or four years older than these young men and young women, Aleksei became a trained and highly regarded seminary teacher during 1993 and 1994. His friendly, ever-cheerful, spiritually dynamic personality endeared him to the students. No one could have guessed the personal sorrows and handicaps that this young leader had overcome.

Aleksei received financial sponsorship from two admiring LDS couples so that he could serve a full-time mission. While awaiting his call, he served as a part-time district missionary. Finally the mission call arrived from the President of the Church. Aleksei could hardly believe it: he was the first Ukrainian Latter-day Saint called to preach the gospel in the United States, and in Utah of all places! Throngs of admirers, young and old, said good-bye as this tall, impressive servant of the Lord left for the Missionary Training Center in Provo, Utah.

Svetlana's Rescue

I will call her Svetlana, although that is not her real name. She always had a strong desire as a young woman to have a successful marriage in which her children could have the happiness that had not existed in her parents' home. Svetlana knew that most Soviet marriages ended in divorce, but she was nevertheless determined to find the right husband and make a happy family.

Years later she found her dreams in shambles. She and her husband were divorced, leaving her to love and raise their son, Sergei, alone, as well as to support them financially. She was determined, however, that she would complete her university education to get a better job and that she would somehow still provide the daily love that her son needed. It proved impossible for her to do this. She had to work all day and attend her education classes in the evenings, leaving no time for Sergei, and she was determined that he would have a loving parent at his side.

Accordingly, she gave up her dreams of higher education and an intelligentsia-status profession, accepting a lesser-paying job that permitted her to be home evenings for Sergei. Economic circumstances were dismal, and Sergei was going through difficult challenges with some of his teenage friends. Two of his close friends had been arrested for breaking the law. Svetlana was doing her best, but was discouraged and fearful that she was failing as a provider and a parent.

Svetlana had heard of The Church of Jesus Christ of Latter-day Saints from one of her friends who had become a member a couple of years earlier. She had always felt, however, that relationships with God should be private, in one's mind and heart, and not a matter of collective institutional worship. For this reason she had not accepted the invitation of her Latter-day Saint friend to visit the Church meetings.

One day as she was worrying and praying about her life and Sergei, an impression came to her to attend a Latter-day Saint meeting with her son. If her son could find a church, perhaps this would help him with his life. The next Sunday they both attended and felt a marvelous witness of the Holy Spirit as they listened to beautiful hymns, saw the sacrament of the Lord's supper administered, and heard testimonies from the pulpit by members of the branch. They both knew this would be their spiritual home.

After meeting and studying with the missionaries for about a month, Svetlana and Sergei were baptized. Sergei's life and his friendships radically changed. He loved associating with the youth of the Church in Sunday meetings and weekday activities. He enthusiastically embraced the high moral and spiritual standards of the Church. The biggest effect upon him, however, was his relationship with the missionaries from America. They were his heroes, and every spare moment he had would be spent proselyting and studying with them.

About eighteen months later, with thanksgiving and tears of both joy and sadness, Svetlana bade farewell to her son, who had received his full-time mission call to serve in Russia. The gospel had rescued both Svetlana and her son.

Viktoria's Choice

A young woman whom I'll call Viktoria grew up in a small town in Ukraine, remaining there until she graduated from secondary school. She was raised solely by her grandmother, who gave her "everything one could give: education, love, care," Viktoria says. "She cultivated in me a taste for spiritual music and art; in short, she gave me the foundation of my spiritual values." Viktoria continues:

> My first steps in this world were made with the help of my grandmother. I remember that time very well, and I remember that we never talked about God. My grandmother lived in a time when it was forbidden to talk about these things; therefore, she did not know anything about God. We did not have the Bible, but I heard of Jesus Christ, although, of course, I did not understand anything about his mission then.
>
> Now I recall that I have always believed in God, or to speak exactly, I believed in the Supreme Power which ruled the world. I remember how I wanted to pray when I was fourteen or fifteen years old, but I did not know how to do that. I just talked to him like I would to a beloved and close person. Then I learned the prayer, "Our Father Which Art

in Heaven." I felt comfort and joy in offering it, but I did not know that God would answer my prayers to him.

Viktoria was not yet seventeen when she entered a post-secondary program at a theatrical institute in the city. Like other students, she was living on her own in the big city and relishing her independence. She did well in her studies, but as she declares:

> I forgot about my soul. It seemed to me that if I smoked and drank alcohol, I would be closer to the world of theater. I wanted to imitate my new friends. . . . But after several months and many mistakes, I realized that I had lost something. I had lost myself, my pure dreams and great hopes.
>
> I gave up painting, listening to music, writing poems. I began to feel not at home in my world. I began to hate myself for losing my innocence. Like many young people, I asked, "What shall I do? What is it all for? What am I living for?" Then I started to pray again, but in this case I wanted forgiveness. I did not know that I could repent. I remember that I felt good after prayers. My prayers were just talking to God.

After a spat with her boyfriend, Viktoria met an acquaintance on the way back to her living quarters who invited her to attend Latter-day Saint church services on Sunday. She began attending but did not understand much at all. When she started listening to the missionary discussions, Viktoria again became confused. For eight months she was taught various times by different missionaries, but still she could not decide what she believed and what she would commit herself to do.

Then one night Viktoria dreamed she was in a forest. As she describes it:

> I had an eagle sitting on my left shoulder and a white dove on my right shoulder. The eagle was playing with me, but the dove warned me not to look at the eagle. I woke up and the knowledge came to me that the dove was the Holy Ghost, and the eagle was the spirit of the Evil One. They

*Ukrainian Elder
Aleksei Kopeigora bids
farewell to his sister
before departing to the
Missionary Training
Center in Provo, Utah,
1994.*

were fighting for my soul, and I understood that I had to
make a choice. I felt such a great joy and a sense of peace,
for the choice was clear to me.

The next Sunday there were very powerful testimonies
borne in the church. Everyone was crying for joy. The Holy
Ghost descended upon all of us. After the meeting I ran
to Elder Ericson and really cried, saying I wanted to be
baptized.

After a period of preparation, Viktoria was baptized in the
nearby river. "It was the most precious day of my life," she
recalls. "It was the beginning of a new life for me. I remembered how I had wanted God to answer my prayers. Now I felt
a forgiveness and joy that I cannot describe. I became happier
every day. My Church friends' example helped me so much.
The missionaries were such a wonderful example to me."

Viktoria's decision to be baptized was, indeed, the beginning of a new life for her. Today she has an eternal temple
marriage. She has completed her university studies. All these
blessings started from her crucial decision to accept Jesus
Christ and his "great plan of happiness" (Alma 42:8).

The Lord's Champion

Vasya is a tall, athletic, blond young man. He had recently
graduated from the Institute of Sport when he encountered
The Church of Jesus Christ of Latter-day Saints.

111

In the Soviet Union athletics were taken very seriously, not only for health and recreational reasons but also because of their political value. The Institute of Sport was given lavish financial and professional training resources to find and train super world-class athletes in every sport, to demonstrate the superiority of the "socialist way of life."

Tennis was a relatively new sport in the Soviet Union. It had been traditionally viewed as a "decadent bourgeois sport of the richer classes." But that view had changed, and a great effort was being made to train young athletes who would eventually become world-class competitors.

Vasya was one of those recruited to become a world-class performer in the field of tennis. He had done very well at the Institute of Sport. Now he had recently made a great breakthrough at Amsterdam, defeating two major European competitors, including a top-ranked tennis star in the Netherlands. It appeared that his career was launched.

Some of Vasya's friends at the Institute of Sport, including his close tennis friend, Denis, became interested in meeting with Latter-day Saint missionaries from America. Their interest attracted Vasya as well. He appreciated the attitudes of young Church members toward the disciplined care of the physical body, and their high moral standards regarding honesty and chastity impressed him.

Ukrainian and Russian sportsmen avoided alcohol and tobacco when they were in training. Yet, at other times, Vasya noted, they gave into these practices so traditional in their society. Vasya had no desire to abuse his body at all by partaking of such vices. In his opinion, the Church's revelation known as the Word of Wisdom and its doctrine concerning the body as a temple of God provided profound moral, spiritual, and health reasons for a disciplined lifestyle. The expectation that Latter-day Saints will live a life of complete honesty, integrity, and chastity conformed to Vasya's own personal creed.

Vasya read the Book of Mormon and became convinced

Elder Vasya Osipenko from Ukraine is greeted by leaders at the Missionary Training Center in London, England, in preparation for his mission to Russia.

that it was the word of God, in harmony with the Bible, and that Joseph Smith was a prophet of God. He accepted the challenge of Elder John Lunt and Elder Robert Curnutt to be baptized. Several of his friends in the Institute of Sport were also baptized, including Denis. Vasya's parents were not baptized but enthusiastically supported his decision to become a Latter-day Saint. Denis's brothers and parents joined him in baptism into the Church.

In the Church, Vasya became a popular leader in the Young Single Adult program and an active participant in the institute of religion. He was continually impressed with the way that Latter-day Saint young people lived the high standards of their religion.

Then he was called to be a district missionary. District missionaries were trained by the full-time missionaries in both finding and teaching investigators and in fellowshipping new members. They learned the six missionary discussions for investigators, as well as the fellowshipping discussions for new members.

Vasya was one of thirty district missionaries in Kiev. He brought a number of other young men and women into the Church and in the process developed a strong desire to serve a full-time mission. His parents committed themselves to providing financial support for him, although they lacked the resources to support a mission in Europe or America.

Vasya received an offer to be affiliated with a prestigious tennis association in Western Europe, which would provide him opportunities to compete with topflight world competition and to live in the West. He would have to turn down his mission call to accept this offer, but there was never any question that Vasya would accept the call of the prophet of God above all other things. He did so enthusiastically and without regrets.

Vasya was called to the Russia Moscow Mission. He has been an outstanding missionary and has served as a branch president there, baptizing a number of converts into the Church. Then he was called as an assistant to the mission president.

Although Vasya shows promise of becoming a superior professional athlete and coach, he shows even greater promise of becoming a worthy champion of the Lord Jesus Christ.

"Youth of the Noble Birthright, Carry On!"

The restored gospel has been particularly appealing to youth and young adults in Ukraine, Belarus, and Russia. They love the clarity, optimism, and idealism of the Savior's great plan of happiness. They love the high moral standards of the gospel, which they often contrast to the dominant practices in their societies. They model themselves after the full-time missionaries who brought them the gospel, yet they are proud of their own national heritage.

In every case when we baptized unmarried youth under the age of eighteen, we were thrilled to see at least one of their parents also being baptized. Many young single adults ages eighteen to thirty were baptized. In addition, a number of adult converts were accompanied by their dependent children in baptism into the Church.

The Church Educational System offered perhaps the most spiritually meaningful experience for youth and young adult converts. More than 200 young people in Kiev were enrolled

Elder Robert K. Dellenbach of the Seventy and Sister Biddulph bid farewell to a Ukrainian sister departing on her mission to Russia, 1994.

in seminary and institute of religion classes during its first year, 1993 to 1994, with more than 155 receiving completion diplomas in May 1994. In the second year, according to reports, more than 400 were enrolled. Local instructors were excellently trained by Elder Max Moffett and Sister Elaine Moffett, Church education missionaries serving under the direction of Elder and Sister Frank Hirschi in the Frankfurt area office.

Young men and women enjoyed seminary and other regular activities in their individual branches, and they joined together monthly in the "Kiev Super Saturday" activities. Hundreds of youth also participated regularly in branch, district, and larger youth activities throughout Kiev.

Young Latter-day Saints in Ukraine, Belarus, and Russia enjoy putting on impromptu skits, keeping everyone laughing and clapping. They also enjoy dances but prefer group dancing, in which all holding hands to form a circle, or individual dancing, in contrast to the Western practice of dancing with a single partner. In such dancing, no one need sit on the sidelines.

All youth love cultural group activities, such as attending an opera, symphony, ballet, or an exhibit at an art museum.

They also stage choral and instrumental musical events, theater plays, and art display events in their church buildings. At Christmas and Easter they put together a huge celebration. Church sports organized on a weekly basis, such as Saturday softball, basketball, soccer, and swimming, are also popular.

Church firesides in the former Soviet Union are called "evenings." Periodically "standards evenings" are held, in which the pamphlet *For the Strength of Youth* is discussed by the youth and their leaders. Members strongly support each other in living the high standards of their faith. Youth summer camping activities had started by 1994. In Kiev, where the number of Latter-day Saints was greater than any other city in Ukraine, there was no other religious confession that had as wide a range of spiritual, educational, cultural, social, and athletic activities for young people as the LDS Church.

In 1993 the first all-Ukrainian Latter-day Saint youth conference took place in Kiev, with nearly four hundred youth coming from three cities for the three-day event. Elder Hans B. Ringger of the Seventy, area president, participated in the conference. General sessions, a testimony meeting, workshops, artistic events, athletic events, a picnic, a large service project (which attracted the local media), and a dance were featured. A snake dance of hundreds of youth dressed in national costume made its way down an ancient street in the old quarter of the city.

As is the case throughout the world, young Latter-day Saints in Ukraine, Russia, and Belarus love to be together. They love visits by General Authorities. In Kiev it has become traditional for young women and young men to dress in national costume when they greet visiting General Authorities at the airport with the ancient ritual of "Bread and Salt."

During the years 1992 through 1994, approximately thirty young members of the Church in Kiev served full-time missions. These calls were predominantly to other Russian-speaking missions, such as Moscow, St. Petersburg, Riga, Samara, Novosibirsk, Donetsk, and Rostov; but some were to

LDS youth in national costume greet Elder Hans B. Ringger of the Seventy, Sister Helen Ringger, Elder Neal A. Maxwell of the Quorum of the Twelve, and Sister Colleen Maxwell with the traditional greeting of "bread and salt" at Kiev's Borispol International Airport, spring 1993.

the England Manchester, Utah South, Florida Tampa, Utah Salt Lake Temple Square, California Los Angeles, and Korea Pusan Missions. Some even served in Polynesia.

A number of these youth have started to return from their missions, adding great strength to the Church. When a Greek Catholic priest from Western Ukraine who wanted to be taught about our church visited me in 1994, I invited four of these returned missionaries to teach him the gospel in the Ukrainian language in the mission home. He was greatly impressed, even amazed by these splendid Ukrainian returned missionaries. He recognized their mature faith and knowledge of the scriptures.

A successful district missionary program using primarily local young single adults was also launched in Kiev; in Minsk, Belarus; and in other cities of Ukraine. In Kiev there were as many as thirty district missionaries serving at once during 1993 and 1994. They knew the missionary discussions and dressed to missionary standards, including the wearing of name tags. District missionaries came to be relied upon more and more to assist in proselyting as the number of full-time foreign missionaries who could obtain visas declined during 1994 and 1995.

A Pivotal Event

One inspirational event in early 1994 showed the mettle of these district missionaries. The twelve American full-time missionaries working in Odessa were notified by authorities that they must leave Ukraine immediately and obtain new visas before returning. It was estimated that this would take thirty days, if everything went well.

The twelve full-time missionaries left Odessa and arrived in Kiev on an overnight train. As these elders and sisters prepared to leave Ukraine (temporarily, we hoped), they came into my office and reported how sad they were to be leaving twenty-five investigators in Odessa who had committed to be baptized during the coming month and who were in varying stages of readiness.

I cheered them considerably by bringing ten Ukrainian young adults into the office to meet them. These youth had been well trained in proselyting skills and were veteran district missionaries. These young men and women had agreed to donate up to thirty days of their time to go to Odessa, live in the full-time missionaries' apartments there, and teach all the investigator appointments of each set of departing missionaries. These ten young Ukrainians correlated carefully with the twelve outgoing American missionaries and left that same evening for Odessa, committed to teach and baptize the twenty-five people who were preparing for baptism there.

Nearly thirty days later, Colleen and I visited these young Ukrainian district missionaries in Odessa. They had worked diligently and wisely. Twenty-three of the twenty-five investigators had been successfully prepared by them for baptism. I interviewed these twenty-three candidates, and they were all baptized. In addition, the Ukrainian district missionaries had generated a number of new investigators for the American full-time missionaries, who returned a few days later to their assignments in Odessa.

We had a marvelous zone conference with these ten young Ukrainian missionaries, several of whom had already submitted their papers to go on full-time missions in the near future. The Spirit of the Lord was poured out upon them as they participated in the training sessions, the testimony meeting, and the individual interviews of the conference. Their faith, their zeal, their trust in the Lord, and their skills greatly moved me. All expressed a great gratitude to the Lord and a fervent desire to serve a full-time mission.

They had handled this demanding situation as well as the best full-time elders and sisters in the mission could have done. I was so proud of them! It was then that I realized with joy that the future of the Church in Ukraine is secure and bright. No matter what might happen, the *youth of the noble birthright* are prepared to *carry on!* (see *Hymns,* no. 255).

Chapter 11

THE BLESSINGS
OF OBEDIENCE

*"Consider on the blessed and happy state of
those that keep the commandments of God.
For behold, they are blessed in all things, both
temporal and spiritual."*

—Mosiah 2:41

*"Seek ye first the kingdom of God, and his
righteousness; and all these things shall be
added unto you."*

—Matthew 6:33

A short time after we arrived in Kiev, I was interviewed by a
prominent journalist named Sergei Kiselev, who was the chief
Ukrainian correspondent of *Literaturnaya gazeta* (*Literary
Gazette*), the newspaper of the intelligentsia throughout what
was then the Soviet Union. Having heard that the Mormons
were already in Kiev, Mr. Kiselev wanted to explore with me
the future prospects of The Church of Jesus Christ of Latter-
day Saints in Ukraine. We had some thoughtful discussions
together in my office.

These interviews resulted in a sizable article in which he
carefully and fairly analyzed the teachings and practices of the
LDS Church. In the article he concluded that Ukrainians and
other Eastern Slavic peoples would not find Mormonism
appealing, either in a doctrinal sense or in the high standards
of conduct expected of members of the Church. Kiselev
believed that Ukrainians would find Mormon doctrines like

"moral agency" and "man is that he might have joy" (see 2 Nephi 2:25) too optimistic about human possibilities for the Slavic soul steeped in the Orthodox tradition of suffering and the terrible experiences of Communism. He also felt that Mormon standards regarding sexual behavior; marriage; abstinence from abortion, alcohol, tobacco, tea, coffee, and narcotics—as well as the practices of tithing and fasting—would be personally too demanding for Slavic traditions and would enjoy little appeal among Ukrainians and Russians. He forecast failure for Mormon attempts to proselyte in Ukraine and in other Eastern Slavic countries.

Three years after Kiselev's article, it is already possible to say definitively that the prediction of this thoughtful, learned correspondent was wrong. The Church of Jesus Christ of Latter-day Saints has had an impressive beginning in Ukraine as well as in other successor states of the former Soviet Union. He was particularly wrong about the doctrinal appeal of the restored gospel. The written accounts and testimonies of countless converts show that people who had experienced terrible suffering were looking for the promise of joy. They were searching for the "great plan of happiness" from the Lord (Alma 42:8). Moral agency was a new doctrine to those who had known only the Orthodox tradition, but it was embraced enthusiastically by most investigators who encountered the Church.

Kiselev was correct, nevertheless, in observing that there would be some difficult social and cultural barriers for would-be converts to Mormonism in the Eastern Slavic countries. He identified some, but not all, of these barriers of tradition.

The high standards of the law of chastity, the Word of Wisdom, tithing, Sabbath observance, and the law of the fast were readily accepted in theory by those who desired to spiritually change their lives. At the level of practice, however, powerful social traditions and serious economic circumstances made the observance of these commandments a great test of faith.

The use and abuse of alcohol is a powerful ancient tradition in this land, especially among men. Even for those who do not abuse alcohol, social drinking is an important part of family gatherings, holidays, and festivals, of which there are many on the calendar. The Soviets established a whole parallel calendar of holidays to counteract and draw people away from the church holidays. Now in the post-Soviet era, the people celebrate both sets of holidays, and heavy drinking binges are a central feature in all of them.

Alcohol abuse is not only a social tradition but also a manifestation of social alienation. Habitual abuse is an escape from grinding, unhappy circumstances and an expression of hopelessness. Increasing personal alienation from society during the Soviet era and the economic and social collapse during the post-Soviet era have greatly increased the incidence of alcohol abuse. It is clearly evident even to the casual observer that alcohol use and abuse is much higher in Russia, Ukraine, and Belarus than in Western countries.

It is also the tradition for almost everyone to use tobacco heavily, even more so than in Western Europe. The social tradition of drinking tea is universal, comparable to that of Britain. Narcotic use is growing but probably remains lower than in the United States.

Undeniably the Word of Wisdom has been one of the most difficult barriers for would-be converts to overcome. That so many have successfully overcome deep habits of substance abuse is a manifestation of the great faith of the people.

The Healing Power of Christ

I will call him Vladimir, although that is not his real name. He was thirty-six years of age when he wrote the following account of his conversion. He had been married thirteen years, was the father of two children, and was a plumber by profession. His story, unfortunately, is not unique, but it demonstrates the faith of many brethren who have changed their lives as they have come to the restored gospel.

122

Kiev: Some of the first group of Seminary and Institute of Religion graduates in spring 1994 with Elder Dennis B. Neuenschwander of the Seventy and President Biddulph.

I had many quarrels and fights in my family. I was a heavy drinker of alcohol, a very heavy smoker, and I was seriously ill. After having three operations in three years, the doctors at Shalimov Institute said I needed one more operation, but I refused.

I knew that there was a God above, but I did not know what to do. Then I started to pray, but I still drank heavily. My prayers did not help me, and I found myself in the hospital again. Still my smoking and drinking continued.

Vladimir then describes how he and his wife met Elder James Karper and Elder Tyson Richardson, how they visited Church services, and how they listened to the missionary discussions. They accepted the gospel and desired to be baptized. Their baptismal date was set, but Vladimir could not seem to overcome his habits, so the date had to be postponed several times.

He returned to the hospital very ill. Elder Karper and Elder Richardson visited his room, blessed him, and promised that the power of Christ would help him overcome his terrible addictions. He was told Christ would make him victorious if he believed and would do all in his power. Vladimir remembers that he was promised that one day he not only would be a member of the Church but also would hold the priesthood and would baptize his daughter.

> Tearfully, I made a sacred resolve to live the Word of Wisdom, and I repented that night of my sins. Immediately I began to feel better the next morning. I was so eager for my baptism that I cannot describe how much I desired it. Finally, this wonderful day came, and I was happier than on any other day of my life. I was baptized on January 3, 1993.
>
> I felt better every day. My faith was strengthened and I was growing spiritually. When I took my medical examination, the doctors were surprised to find that I was completely healthy. I bore my testimony to the doctor about Christ, that he lives and had saved me from death. The doctor was not happy with my words, grumbling that the medicine had made me well, but I told him that I had not taken any of the medicine he had given me.
>
> My soul was filled with great joy. I thanked my Heavenly Father for accepting me into his kingdom and for saving me from death. The gospel has changed my life completely. I have become quite another person. Now, more than one year later, I am not ill, and I need no medicines. I feel very good. Like Elder Karper promised me, I have received the priesthood, and I baptized my daughter. I have baptized my whole family into the Kingdom of God.

Valentina's Faith

Valentina is a senior citizen who had drunk strong coffee for several years as a prescription from her doctor for a health condition. When she was preparing for baptism into The Church of Jesus Christ of Latter-day Saints, Valentina read of the Word of Wisdom and what it said about coffee. She returned to her doctor and asked if there might be a prescription that would permit her to take something other than coffee for her condition. The doctor said that he knew of nothing available and that if that were true she should continue drinking the coffee. She scoured the woefully depleted pharmacies throughout the city and found that there were no other stimulants available that would meet her needs.

Valentina might have concluded that in the absence of other remedies she was justified in taking coffee purely for medicinal purposes, as her doctor prescribed. It troubled her, however, to fail to fulfill anything given of the Lord. "I don't want to miss any of the spiritual blessings the Lord has promised in this revelation. I want to be an example to my family, who are all unbelievers. How can I do that if they see me drink coffee each day?"

After prayerful consideration, Valentina approached the missionaries who had taught her the gospel. "If you will give me a blessing through the priesthood, I believe Heavenly Father will take away my health problems. Whatever his will might be, however, I have decided that I will never drink tea or coffee again. I trust in the words of our Savior."

Valentina received a wonderful blessing, promising her health and spiritual gifts through her faith. She was then baptized, and immediately her health problem disappeared. She has often publicly borne her testimony about this experience and of the spiritual and temporal blessings that the Lord granted her through obedience to his commandments.

Blessings of the Sabbath

Hyperinflation in the Ukrainian economy has caused prices of necessities like food to skyrocket. More and more of the food distributed in the cities is available only in the private markets, where the prices are much higher than in state outlets. The result is that only a few city dwellers can afford to buy all of their fresh food requirements. They must either rent garden spots far outside the city to produce their own food or arrange for a family member or friend who lives in a rural area to help them with food. Old people who lack the health, mobility, or connections to the rural areas live only slightly above starvation.

They are able to afford to buy bread and little else. Even

bread prices skyrocket faster than old-age pensions, leaving those without access to rural garden plots less and less able to feed themselves.

I will call him Anatoly. He lives with his wife, whom I shall call Yulia, and two children in a major Ukrainian city. Anatoly and Yulia rented cheaply from the state a large garden plot, approximately sixty-five kilometers from the city. They erected a small dwelling to stay in while they worked the land. Under the floorboards of the home they dug a root cellar to store the potatoes, carrots, onions, squash, cabbage, beets, and turnips harvested on the land. They also raised more perishable crops, such as tomatoes and cucumbers.

Anatoly's family enjoys "going to the dacha" on week-ends, as they call it. They enjoy the fresh air, the quiet rural environment, and the benefits of physical labor together in the out-of-doors. While this activity is a pleasant diversion, it is also essential for the family's well-being. If they did not raise and store vegetables for the winter, they would not be able to afford to live as a family of four (considered large in the for-mer Soviet Union).

Before they received the restored gospel, Anatoly, Yulia, and the children traveled to their plot of land by bus (they have no car) for two hours on Friday after work and school had finished, returning late on Sunday evening. This gave them all day Saturday and Sunday to work the land, from early spring to late fall (seven months of the year). Every week throughout the year, however, they would make the trip just to gather and haul bags of food from their root cellar to last them the following week in the city.

Anatoly, Yulia, and their children received the gospel with great joy. One of the commandments of the Lord, however, is the law of the Sabbath. They learned of the importance of going to the house of prayer on the Lord's day to partake of the sacrament in renewal of their covenants with the Lord, to study his holy word, and to serve others in various callings.

It would not be difficult to observe the Sabbath day in the

Spring 1994. District and branch presidents from eight cities in Ukraine host Alexander Litvinov (front row, black shirt without collar), representative for religious affairs in the Cabinet of Ministers of Ukraine.

winter season, for they could gather food on Saturdays and return to the city before the Sabbath. Being in the city on Sunday for church and for other callings during the growing season, however, would mean giving up one of the two precious days each week set aside for the essential work on the garden plot.

Anatoly was in a quandary. Had not the Lord given him the responsibility of providing for his family? Yes, he was sure of it. Yet the Lord had also given him the commandment to attend Church meetings and serve him on the Sabbath. How could he fulfill both of these commandments? He could not change his work schedule in the city. If he gave one of the two precious days allotted for feeding his family to the Lord, would he still be able to provide for his family?

Yulia and Anatoly were taught by the missionaries that the Lord never gives a commandment without providing a way for it to be fulfilled (see 1 Nephi 3:7). They were told of the promises of bountiful blessings if they would observe the Sabbath.

Anatoly and Yulia were counseled to do what was necessary to provide for their family, but if they were committed to the Sabbath and prayed for the opportunity to observe it, a way would be provided without hurting their temporal welfare. They had their own agency as well as their responsibility before the Lord to decide themselves what they should do in every situation.

Anatoly and Yulia decided that they would honor the Sabbath day and actively serve in the Church, as well as provide for their family. They were baptized together as a family. When the growing season came, however, at first they sometimes felt the necessity to stay in the country to work on Sundays.

After a few months, however, they realized that their garden was growing just as well on the weeks when they returned home Saturday evening as it did when they stayed one more day. From that time forward, they were always in church and serving others on the Sabbath.

Some time later they bore public testimony of the temporal and spiritual blessings received from honoring the Sabbath and of the bounteous harvest of food with which the Lord had blessed them. Anatoly said that his tomatoes were better that year than they had ever been before. Yulia said their garden plot was known by others in the area to be more bountiful than any of the plots surrounding it. With tears in their eyes and emotion in their voices, Anatoly and Yulia bore witness in the branch fast and testimony meeting. "We know the promises of the Lord about the Sabbath are true! We know his gospel is true, that he loves us and will bless us."

The following year that same garden plot provided ample food not only for their family but also for three elderly widows and one of the widows' granddaughters, solely through the labor of Anatoly's family, given only on Saturdays.

A Blessing from the Windows of Heaven

I will call her Viktoria. She is a middle-aged, single parent with two teenage children. She has worked for years at a menial occupation. Her wages are meager and her family lives in poverty in a small, one-room, broken-down apartment on the seventh floor of an old building without an elevator.

Viktoria's work was in a building where a branch of the Church meets in a Ukrainian city. She had received some religious training as a child but had spent most of her life without any spiritual environment. She would often stop her work and sit on the back row of the Sunday meetings. When one day a missionary invited her to hear the gospel discussions, she accepted.

Viktoria had a strong spiritual witness of the truth of the Book of Mormon as she read it. She found the missionary discussions filled with meaning for her. She was preparing to be baptized.

The law of tithing was the big hurdle of faith for Viktoria. Her low wage and the hyperinflation put her in a desperate economic situation. How could she continue to buy food? How would she clothe her children? They were badly in need of winter coats and boots, but there was no money for this. Her son was ill, needing hospital care. Her daughter had a spinal condition that needed correction while she was growing. Now she learned that Mormons believe in freely giving one-tenth of their income to the Lord. How would it be possible?

Members of the Church believe in voluntarily donating one-tenth of their income to the Lord. Those donated funds are used solely within the country where they are given to fulfill the spiritual and humanitarian needs of the Church. There is no soliciting of tithes. People give voluntarily and confidentially. Church leaders and officers are not financially supported by the Church and are not paid out of tithes for their service. All Church service is freely given.

Viktoria prayed to the Lord about all her problems and about tithing. She acknowledged her acceptance of his gospel and her desire to fulfill every commandment of God. What should she do? Again she felt the spiritual impression to accept the restored gospel. This time she felt a peaceful, burning

129

assurance that the Lord would bless her temporally and spiritually if she voluntarily accepted his commandments.

The scheduled date of her baptism was only two or three days away. Viktoria came to church that Sunday, deciding that she would freely but confidentially offer her first tithe to the Lord. A few days later she was offered additional employment that was compatible with her work schedule and her family needs. It paid significantly more than the other job and involved fewer hours. It nearly tripled her income.

Soon Viktoria had enough money to buy the coats, the boots, and the clothing needed. The medical needs of her children were taken care of in the succeeding period. From time to time, there arose other needs that she could not financially meet. She would kneel and pray for help, and always some miracle occurred that solved the problem. Usually the help came anonymously, but it always came at the right moment and without her asking any human agent for help.

Viktoria came to my office to express her testimony of tithing and her love of the Church. I shall not forget her strong, sweet testimony: "I have proved the Lord's promises concerning tithing. I know it is a true commandment and that the Lord blesses those who have faith sufficient to live it. I love the Lord and his true Church." At this her eyes filled with tears of conviction and joy.

"Seek Ye First the Kingdom of God"

There is a severe housing crisis in Ukraine and other successor states of the former Soviet Union. Even divorced spouses cannot easily immediately separate their living quarters. Alcohol-related physical abuse of wife and children by a husband is the most common problem associated with family breakup, but often because of lack of accommodations, the family must continue to tolerate his presence for an extended period.

The government tries to solve this problem by giving to divorced spouses highest priority for new apartments. Married people, however, are also desperately trying to get better and larger apartments as their family grows. Since they know that divorcées receive preferential positions on waiting lists for housing, many married couples are tempted to get a legal divorce and then continue living together in order to get a desperately needed apartment.

The temptation for two spouses who love each other to obtain a legal divorce in order to get an additional apartment is even greater now that the Ukrainian government is privatizing many of these state apartments and giving them to tenants free of charge. There is a lucrative real-estate market in U.S. dollars in Ukrainian cities. Receiving an additional apartment is, therefore, an enormous gift for a Ukrainian.

There are some churches that allegedly perform secret marriage ceremonies, not reported to the government, so that a couple who are legally registered as divorced or as single may live together, "married in the eyes of God," even while they are pretending otherwise to the government.

The Church of Jesus Christ of Latter-day Saints, of course, will not condone such a practice. In order to qualify for baptism, couples living together must show legal proof that they are married in the eyes of the government. This evidence is noted officially on their current domestic passport. If not, they must be married or remarried with a government registration of this act before they may join the Church.

Once remarried in the eyes of the law, however, these tenants automatically lose their priority position on the endless list to get a new apartment. This means that such a couple must postpone indefinitely their hopes for a new, better apartment in order to be baptized into the Church.

This is a hard test of faith for a baptismal candidate. Such a situation forces a couple to make a wrenching choice between the Lord and even meager material things of the world, between chastity and unchastity, between honesty and dishonesty. Many are not yet ready to give up such a material opportunity in exchange for the gospel.

I have known quite a few families in such a situation, however, who after prayer and soul-searching have returned to my office with the peace of the gospel glowing on their faces, their eyes full of joy, and a marriage registration stamped on their passport.

I always asked such couples who returned after freely deciding to reregister their marriage so that they could be baptized: "What brought you to this decision?" And quite frequently they point to one of the scriptures I had previously asked them to ponder and pray about: "Then answered Peter and said unto him, Behold, we have forsaken all, and followed thee; what shall we have therefore? And Jesus said unto them, . . . every one that hath forsaken houses . . . or lands, for my name's sake, shall receive an hundredfold, and shall inherit everlasting life" (Matthew 19:27–29).

They often explain that they love the Lord more than the apartment for which they had dreamed. They speak of a feeling that the Lord will bless them both spiritually and temporally if they do the right thing. Whether or not the dream apartment will ever come to pass, they are ready to trust in the blessings and promises of the Lord.

They are ready to receive his kingdom. When this has happened, I reinforce them in the decision they have made, promising them that if they seek first the kingdom of God and his righteousness, all the blessings they need will be added in the Lord's due time (see Matthew 6:33). Then I have always offered to give them a blessing by the laying on of hands. The Lord has attended these blessings with a marvelous outpouring of the Spirit. These were precious experiences I can never forget.

I can never forget the wonderful faith with which Ukrainians, Belarussians, and Russians have overcome the cultural and economic obstacles to their entrance into the kingdom of God. In forsaking all, they are heirs to the incomprehensibly great blessings of their spiritual father, Abraham.

Chapter 12

THINGS LOVELY
AND PRAISEWORTHY

"If there is anything virtuous, lovely, or of good report or praiseworthy, we seek after these things."

—Articles of Faith 1:13

"The artist is given a holy gift of creation, in the likeness of the creative power of the Eternal Father. It must not be misused or cheapened. True art is a form of revelation. It has always been so for me. I have awakened in the night with a vision before my mind of exactly what was to be created and how it would be done."

—Anatoly Krisochenko, LDS Ukrainian artist

No people support, love, and cherish the arts more than the Ukrainians. Those who are accomplished in artistic expression are publicly acclaimed in much the same manner that athletes are in the West. A number of professionals working in a variety of artistic fields have been attracted to accept the restored gospel, especially in Kiev. These include vocalists, pianists and other instrumental soloists, composers, ballet dancers, actresses and actors in the theater, painters, sculptors, and illustrators, as well as others. I will present the spiritual odyssey of a few of these converts to The Church of Jesus Christ of Latter-day Saints.

World Medalist Accepts the Gospel

Arkady Orokhovsky was born in the small Ukrainian town of Kamenets-Podolsky in 1969. He was not brought up with any religious training by his parents, but his devout grandmother taught him about personal worship and took him to visit churches.

Arkady's talent as a dancer was recognized early, and his parents brought him to Kiev at age ten to study at a ballet and choreography school for talented children. He was the only student in this choreography school to be ultimately chosen for a professional career in the magnificent Opera House of Ukraine in Kiev. Early in 1988, before turning nineteen, he was chosen as a solo ballet dancer with the Ukrainian National Academic Theater of Opera and Ballet, a noted opera house named in honor of Taras Shevchenko, a former serf who became Ukraine's most famous poet.

As a member of this most elite ballet ensemble in Ukraine, Arkady participated as a solo dancer regularly in the opera house in Kiev, as well as in performances around the world: in many European countries, Canada, the United States, Latin America, and Japan. The skill and reputation of this tall, athletic young man in his early twenties developed rapidly.

Arkady met Galina in 1990. Galina had just finished her candidate of sciences degree (Ph.D.) in Russian Language and Literature at Kiev State University and had been hired as a professor at the Institute of Higher Qualification, which trains and certifies teachers of Russian and Ukrainian languages throughout the republic. Galina also is fluent in both English and Spanish. She is a native of Kiev, the daughter of a history professor who lost his academic position and career for refusing to join the Communist Party.

Like her parents, Galina was also fiercely independent of any connection with the party and was a convinced anti-Communist. She began her career, however, at a time of greater intellectual freedom.

World medalist ballet dancer Arkady Orokhovsky (right).

Beyond what we would call the Ph.D., Galina was later admitted in 1993 as a candidate to the doctor of sciences degree, held by only a few top academicians in the country. Her doctoral dissertation was a comparison of Russian novelist Aleksander Solzhenitsyn's *Gulag Archipelago* and Ukrainian writer Ivan Bagryany's *The Garden of Gethsemane*. Both writers had bravely condemned Communism during the Soviet era, yet Galina was permitted to work freely on the interpretation of their writings.

Arkady and Galina were not religious believers at the time they first encountered the Mormons in Kiev during the fall of 1991. At the Institute of Higher Qualification, one of the Russian teachers whom Galina trained was Alla, who with her daughter Viktoria (also an Institute student) had joined the Church in Kiev during the previous summer and had been baptized by Elder Gregory Christiansen. Galina accepted

Alla's invitation to attend Latter-day Saint meetings, which were held in the Ukrainian Writers Union Hall.

Galina returned from the church service very impressed spiritually. She met the young foreign missionaries, most of whom were at fairly early stages in learning to speak the Russian language, although several spoke the language well. These young men and women greatly impressed her spiritually. She met Elder Charles Creel and Sister Susan Creel. She and Arkady were soon giving language lessons to the Creels, who in turn were teaching the gospel to their hosts during the fall of 1991.

Arkady and Galina read the Book of Mormon and received a strong testimony of the restored gospel. As she read and discussed the gospel, Galina was drawn to the doctrine of moral agency and the eternal potential of women and men as literal children of God. She had always rejected both the Communist ideology and the dominant religious theology in her society because their assumptions about man seemed to justify an authoritarian enslavement of human beings. She was excited about the personal dignity and eternal possibilities that the restored gospel confers upon both women and men, the doctrine of eternal families, and the concept of the temple.

Arkady enthusiastically embraced the same optimistic vision of the divine heritage and potential of mankind. He was particularly attracted by the gospel imperative to eternally strive for perfection (see Matthew 5:48) and by the view that human artistic creativity is a sacred power, patterned after our Eternal Father's divine power as a creator.

Arkady and Galina made two very important decisions, which were carried out during December 1991. First, they decided on matrimony and were married on 28 December. Then, on the following day, they both accepted baptism into the Church.

After becoming a member of the Church, Arkady faced a serious dilemma. As a world-class professional, his schedule could not be adjusted to include Sunday church attendance.

He and Galina had only a couple of hours a week on Mondays to discuss and read the gospel together. The ballet ensemble required fourteen-hour days, including Sundays, in practice and performance, and the physical demands on his body of such a schedule were very taxing. In such circumstances, Arkady's spiritual development could not keep pace with that of his wife. During a trip to England in the summer of 1993, Galina was endowed in the London Temple, but Arkady was not ready and lacked even the opportunity to schedule such a trip.

Both Arkady and Galina were excelling in their careers, but they desired a family and the eternal blessings that would depend on Arkady's opportunity to be active in the Church. They prayed earnestly about their concerns, and in 1994 these desires were fulfilled. A few months after her return from the London Temple, Galina became pregnant. This news was a great joy to them. She began making adjustments in her plans in order to concentrate fully on her approaching role of motherhood.

Then Arkady entered a world championship competition in 1994, involving ballet solo dancers from many countries. He finished with a bronze medal as a solo dancer and an over-all ranking of second place in this world-wide competition. This performance gave him world stature and an invitation to the United States to try out for an opening as a principal dancer and ballet master for a ballet company in Texas.

At twenty-four years of age, Arkady was chosen for this position in Texas. Most important, it provided him with suffi-cient time to be active in the Church and to prepare for the temple. Galina gave birth to a son almost immediately after their arrival in America.

Galina and Arkady were deeply grateful to the Lord for answering their prayers and blessing their lives. They are both greatly enjoying parenthood. Along with their son, Stephen, they have begun a new life in Texas, where they are active members of the Church, preparing for eternal temple blessings.

Internationally Acclaimed Artist Finds the Truth

One day Colleen and I were invited by Galina to visit a renowned Ukrainian painter by the name of Anatoly Krisochenko and to view some of his work. Colleen minored in art at Brigham Young University and has continued to paint regularly through the years of our marriage, including in Ukraine during our mission. She was excited to meet a prominent artist whose pictures were in national galleries we had already visited.

Anatoly's home and studio were located on an upper floor of an older apartment building without an elevator in the southwest section of Kiev. As is often the case, the hallways had no light, and so we had to grope our way up unfamiliar stairs in pitch blackness, floor by floor. Fortunately, Colleen had her tiny pocket flashlight for reading numbers on apartment doors.

Finally, on the fourth or fifth floor, we found it—number 41—and rang the bell. We were cordially greeted by a very short man with a mustache, a prominent nose, a full head of gray hair, and large, smiling, dark eyes. He was a man in his seventies who appeared in fragile health but in whose face one could behold a gentle, purposeful vigor. This future Latter-day Saint was obviously a man with a magnificent obsession in his life.

Anatoly's works are found in fifteen museums throughout Ukraine, including the State Museum of Ukrainian Art and the Shevchenko Museum in Kiev. More than four hundred of his individual works are in museums or collections around the world, including the Vatican. Exhibitions of his works have been shown in New York, Chicago, San Francisco, Seattle, and Santa Monica in the United States, as well as in a number of European countries.

We were ushered into his studio, the high walls of which

Internationally acclaimed Ukrainian artist Anatoly Krisochenko.

were filled with his creations: portraits of himself and other family members, landscapes, decorative art, and paintings inspired by world cultural history, legend, folklore, and fantasy. Yet his most impressive achievement seemed to be his amazing easel-miniatures, hundreds of which he kept in his cabinets, done in acrylic paint but framed under glass. A sea of tiny faces gazed out from the confines of single pictures, no more than four inches square, painted in amazing detail and accuracy using a magnifying glass! One prominent art critic, S. Bongart, has written of Anatoly's miniatures:

"This style of painting is a unique and personal art form which is solely Krisochenko's and easily places him in the ranks of the Soviet Union's most gifted and original painters. Krisochenko has created a completely new style of easel-miniatures. . . . Like all genuine art, these works have consistently amazed artists and critics of divergent aesthetic beliefs."

Anatoly told us about his unusual life. He was born on

8 October 1916 in Kiev on the birth date of his father, also an artist. His father was the son of an Orthodox priest and had to hide his own paintings of spiritual subjects to avoid punishment by Communist authorities. His mother was both a painter and a singer. Both encouraged their son's ambition to become an artist.

Anatoly graduated from the Kiev Academy of Art, where many other talented Ukrainian masters of painting had studied. His mentor was the painting master from Moscow, Pyotr Kotov, who also taught and influenced other famous Russian and Ukrainian artists.

Anatoly's wife, Nina, is also an artist, creating lovely pictures made of stitched silk threads. His older son, Nikolai, is a gifted painter; and Anatoly's younger son, Pavel, is a well-known illustrator specializing in Ukrainian warrior uniforms and weapons through the ages. Anatoly and Nikolai often work together on a portrait or landscape. Colleen later watched father and son work together in perfect harmony, with Anatoly supervising and adding the finishing touches to a portrait.

This future Latter-day Saint artist shunned membership in the Communist Party or in the official, party-controlled Artists Union. This greatly curtailed the public acceptance of his work until the 1980s. When necessary to put food on the table, he made pictures and murals of Lenin and other Soviet political subjects, but his preference was to avoid the propaganda art form of "socialist realism," developing his own style and his own themes. Before the Gorbachev era, however, there was no hope of exhibiting any of this rich Ukrainian national art. He was painting, as they say, "for his own drawer."

Colleen particularly loved Anatoly's painting of his mother and later received his permission to paint a copy of it. He watched over her creative effort, gave suggestions, and added some finishing touches himself. In gratitude, she wrote the following poem about Anatoly's painting of his mother, which she gave to him on his baptism day:

Your Face
(To a Ukrainian Mother)

I love to read faces.
Yours offers an intriguing story.
Each wrinkle, curve, and feature
I desire to interpret.
You sit in the garden with lowered head,
half-closed eyes,
a humble countenance,
reflective mood.
The sun highlights your white linen head-covering,
where shades, shadows, and light
play intricate games of fusion and contrast.
I ponder . . .
How many times did you scrub
that linen by hand?
How many rivers of water did you heat
to do the mountains of laundry a family creates?
How many seasons did you toil in the garden
to supply sustenance for hungry loved ones?
How many babes did you croon to sleep?
Whose fevered brow did you cool?
Did you worry, stay up late,
waiting for your young to return?
Old Mother, you were kind.
With delicate, loving strokes of the brush
your artist son depicts that.
He is kind also.
Anatoly learned it, no doubt, from you.
Joy and sorrow, love and pain,
labor and disappointment, spiritual yearnings
—all these carved your face.
You lived a full, long life.
You continue to live through the portrait.
Your face inspires all who would read it.

—Colleen C. Biddulph, 17 June 1992

Anatoly told us he had investigated many religions and philosophies. He himself is a philosopher and spiritual seeker. He showed genuine interest in a copy of the Russian edition of the Book of Mormon that we left for him to read, along with a pamphlet about Joseph Smith. We also invited him to attend church services.

A few days later we were delighted to greet him at church. Two weeks later he brought several of his family members with him to church. We invited them to hear the missionary gospel discussions, and Sister Tania Rands and Sister Melinda Richards taught them the restored gospel. When Anatoly and his son, Nikolai, were ready for baptism, they asked me to perform this sacred ordinance for them in the Dnieper River.

Anatoly was spiritually moved by his reading of the Book of Mormon:

> Because I have studied many religions, when I first heard about the Mormon Church, I was very interested. When I became acquainted with the Book of Mormon, it soon became clear to me who Mormon really was and who Joseph Smith was. Joseph Smith had visions, and it was made known to him where the golden plates were located and that they were holy writings. These plates contained the teachings of Jesus Christ, and on these truths The Church of Jesus Christ of Latter-day Saints is built. After reading that holy record, I am sure that the Mormon Church on the earth today is a continuation of the Church in the ancient days under Christ.

Soon after their baptism, Anatoly and Nikolai, with the help of Pavel, began painting their own illustrations of Book of Mormon themes. Five or six of these had already been completed by mid-1994.

Anatoly's own synthesis of art and religion has guided his life, both before and after the fall of Communism. It has only been enhanced by his reception of the restored gospel of Jesus Christ: "The artist is given a holy gift of creation, in the likeness of the creative power of the Eternal Father. It must not be misused or cheapened. True art is a form of revelation. It has always been so for me. I have awakened in the night with a vision before my mind of exactly what was to be created and how it would be done."

A Heavenly Duet

The third and final story is about Eleonora and her husband, Gennady Aksyutin. Eleonora and Gennady had already retired from nationally prominent careers in the field of music when they found the gospel.

Eleonora had been a nationally famous soprano. During the post-Stalin Soviet era, she performed as a soloist with the leading musical organizations of Ukraine and of the Soviet Union. She made numerous recordings of classical and Ukrainian national music and was publicly acclaimed, being awarded the rare titles "Honored Artist of the USSR" and "Honored Artist of Ukraine," reserved for the premier musical performers of the country.

Gennady is a fine tenor. After a successful professional career, he went into teaching and the field of administration of culture in Ukraine. He was a professor of voice at the Kiev Conservatory of Music and involved with the Ukrainian Ministry of Culture in arranging performance scheduling for the National Opera and National Symphony Orchestra of Ukraine. Later, he was to make all the local arrangements for the Brigham Young University Ballroom Dancers to tour ten major cities of Ukraine in 1994.

This distinguished, cultured couple has had an unusual marriage relationship. Unlike many of their peers in the arts community, Gennady and Eleonora have had a beautiful, loving, mutually supportive marriage for more than forty years, in spite of the pressures of their separate careers. Although greatly desiring children, they were unable to have any, but the gentleness, courtesy, and affection with which they treated each other was a beautiful example to their professional peers and to other members of the Church.

Gifted soprano Eleonora Aksyutina and her husband, Gennady, a renowned tenor.

Eleonora and Gennady were among the many members of the "creative intelligentsia" (*tvorcheskaya intelligentsia*) who became religious seekers in the late 1980s after a lifetime of living without religion. Eleonora took the lead in this search. One day a friend told her about the newly organized branch of the Church, which was meeting on the Left Bank in a prominent drama theater near their apartment.

Eleonora and Gennady attended the church service and were warmly greeted by Elder John Lunt and Elder Robert Curnutt. The couple invited the elders to teach them the gospel in their home. Soon Gennady and Eleonora were baptized and were using their superb musical talents to assist the Church.

They sang solos and duets in their branch and at district conferences and joined other excellent Kiev Latter-day Saint musicians in putting on public holiday concerts before capacity crowds in major music halls in the Ukrainian capital. In annual Christmas and Easter concerts, they not only performed Ukrainian, Russian, and European music but also introduced thousands of music lovers in Kiev, for the first time, to the best of Latter-day Saint sacred music.

Gennady and Eleonora were often joined in concert by Sister Marilyn Anderson, who was a violinist for twenty-seven years with the Utah Symphony. This trio was usually accompanied by my wife, Colleen, on piano or pipe organ. Sister Anderson and her husband, Mark, of Salt Lake City, were on her fourth and his fifth mission for the Church.

Gennady served as a member of the Left Bank branch presidency, and Eleonora served in the Relief Society. Eleonora and Gennady went on the second temple trip of Ukrainians to the Freiberg Germany Temple in the spring of 1993. They were sealed for time and eternity on the very date of their fortieth wedding anniversary.

A year later, Eleonora was diagnosed with a rapidly developing brain cancer. Only a week after Eleonora sang a vocal solo, her magnificent voice was stilled. Two months later she peacefully passed away in the arms of her eternal companion.

Immediately after her death, radio stations in Kiev and Ukraine were announcing her passing, praising her brilliant career, and playing her music. One last time, on the day of her funeral, the national airwaves carried Eleonora's magnificent voice across the wide expanse of the Ukrainian plain as she was laid to rest.

Eleonora was the first Latter-day Saint in Ukraine to pass away after having been endowed and sealed in the temple. Colleen prepared the body of Eleonora for burial in temple clothing, gathering the Relief Society presidents of Kiev to participate with her. She noticed that an item of temple clothing was missing and spent the evening before the funeral sewing this last item for Eleonora. Colleen and these Relief Society sisters rendered much compassionate service to the bereaved family during this difficult time.

In typical Ukrainian style, members of the Church and prominent cultural figures came to pay their respects before the open casket in the Aksyutin apartment and at the cemetery. Flowers brought by these mourners filled the casket and surrounded it in a huge bank of floral colors. A moving service of music and the spoken word at the apartment and at the cemetery gave many prominent individuals of other faiths, as well as members of the Church, their first experience with a Latter-day Saint funeral.

Through all these difficult events, Gennady showed his fellow Latter-day Saints and distinguished non-Mormon friends what love and death mean to a couple sealed for eternity in the house of the Lord. His testimony of eternal marriage, of the immortality of the soul, and of eternal life touched many hearts, both within and outside the Church.

Chapter 13

FELLOWCITIZENS

"Now therefore ye are no more strangers and foreigners, but fellowcitizens with the saints, and of the household of God."

—Ephesians 2:19

"And he [Alma] commanded them that . . . they should look forward with one eye, . . . having their hearts knit together in unity and in love one towards another. . . . And thus they became the children of God."

—Mosiah 18:21–22

Spiritual conversion is first and foremost a personal relationship with God, but it is also the finding of a spiritual home within the religious community of believers who share a commitment to this same new faith. The personal accounts of new Latter-day Saints in Ukraine, Russia, and Belarus show the adjustment process through which converts moved from feeling like "strangers and foreigners" to becoming "fellowcitizens with the saints, and of the household of God" (Ephesians 2:19).

There was little in the cultural traditions of Ukraine, Russia, or Belarus to prepare new converts for the distinctive practices and social community of the LDS Church. The mode of worship, spiritual community, member participation, and lay leadership of the Latter-day Saints differed fundamentally from the liturgy, clergy, and parish life of Orthodoxy; and it also contrasted with participation in the official social organizations of Soviet Communism.

Russian Tsarism presided over a multinational empire of traditional societies in which there were few meaningful opportunities for large-scale social or political participation by the masses. Soviet society permitted a type of "mobilized citizen participation" in the mass social organizations closely directed by the Communist Party (Nicholas Lampert, "Patterns of Participation"). Those who had been officers or activists in the Communist Party, the Young Communist League (Komsomol), the professional and trade unions, and other official organizations acquired administrative and managerial experience and developed their organizational, overseeing, and communication skills. The absence of a civil society, however, meant that there was no genuine experience of autonomous grassroots participation in Soviet society.

In the Stalin era, moreover, the forced collaboration of many people with the secret police in the mass repression and state-sponsored terror against millions of citizens made everyone fearful of spontaneous social participation and extremely distrustful of all but their most intimate friends. Until the time of Gorbachev in the late 1980s, not only was religious participation considered highly deviant, but any form of volunteer charitable or other autonomous social activity was illegal. Only the state bureaucracy could administer aid or assistance to the needy. Only official organizations controlled by the Communist Party could engage in significant social purposes.

As a consequence, Soviet society produced a people who were highly distrustful and cut off from the personal lives of one another. While citizens from the professional and managerial strata had developed leadership and communication skills, all lacked the experience of truly voluntary social participation, cooperation, and mutual aid.

How could a people with such a background adapt to a

Branch picnic in Minsk, Belarus.

church like that of the Latter-day Saints? Could they establish the close-knit community of brotherhood and sisterhood characteristic of Latter-day Saints elsewhere? Could they effectively support a church totally dependent upon the voluntary participation of all members? Would they learn to trust and loyally support each other in leadership callings? Could enough people be found with spiritual leadership qualities to minister to the rapidly growing number of branches?

I consider it miraculous that a people who had experienced the alien, inhumane circumstances of Soviet society for three-quarters of a century could make so successfully the spiritual and social transition to the Latter-day Saint community of loving service. It is a testimony of the transforming power of the Holy Spirit. The change is not easy for many and incomplete for some, as we shall see, but the final overall result is truly miraculous and beautiful.

The Response to LDS Worship

The vast majority of new Latter-day Saints had not been actively involved in other churches before their baptism. Perhaps this is the reason that only a few of them expressed any reluctance to give up the elaborate liturgy of the traditional churches.

The opinion of a young adult convert named Oksana is typical of many others who joined the Church: "The dominant churches never attracted me. I found no answers or even discussion of religious questions there. All those candles, icons, and cathedrals seemed black and frightening to me." By contrast, in the Latter-day Saint worship service, "there were young, beautiful people who showed me how to love God, and that He loves us and takes care of us."

Aleksei, a middle-aged convert, expressed a similar view:

> The worship service of the traditional churches is designed to produce an overwhelming feeling of fear and awe of God. It is a dark feeling that I have always rejected as the opposite of what God is really like. I always expected that the feeling of God's presence would bring light and new understanding, joy, love, and peace. That is exactly the feeling I had every time I met with the missionaries. It is exactly the feeling I experienced each Sabbath day that I visited the worship services of The Church of Jesus Christ of Latter-day Saints. Since my baptism I have come to recognize that this wonderful feeling is the spiritual enlightenment of the Holy Ghost.

Vyacheslav had long been an atheist. He had functioned as a professional public lecturer and propagandist for the Communist Party during the Soviet era. After the fall of Communism, he began to investigate Protestant Christianity and attended the meetings and lectures of American and Ukrainian evangelists. He comments:

> I could not take the liturgy of the traditional churches seriously. It was an ancient magnificent pageantry, worthy

Choir sings at tri-district conference of the Church in Kiev. Leaders on the stand (from left to right) include district president Aleksander Manzhos (conducting); Elder Dennis B. Neuenschwander of the Seventy; Elder Dallin H. Oaks of the Quorum of theTwelve; Elder C. Max Caldwell of the Seventy; President and Sister Biddulph; district president Gulko; and district president Stavichenko.

of cultural preservation, but not spiritually meaningful to me.

The Protestant evangelists, on the other hand, were trained, talented orators of the gospel who could move the masses. Because of my former training I was, perhaps, a bit cynical about the techniques of skilled religious preachers and found it difficult, therefore, to accept the message of the evangelists, although I found their methods of mass persuasion fascinating.

It was the Mormon worship service that spiritually moved me for the first time in my life. Here I found no ancient liturgy, no religious orators, or even professional clergy. Ordinary people came out of the audience to give short talks which humbly expressed their ideas and feelings about such topics as faith in Jesus Christ, repentance, and love of other people. They had a different kind of eloquence—not of the professional speaker, but of the humble, sincere believer, filled with faith.

I had never before heard people of our own country express themselves like this. Their simple messages penetrated the hard shell of my cynicism and greatly moved me. The following week I visited my first fast and testimony meeting, in which members spontaneously expressed their experiences with God and his blessings to them. I left this meeting touched in the core of my being, hungering for that same blessing in my own life.

It took four more months of deep study and critical discussion, but finally Vyacheslav was at peace with the Spirit, ready for baptism.

New Latter-day Saints continued to cherish the cultural heritage of their national religious art, and a few members of the Church were even professors or instructors in Ukrainian or Russian culture and docents in museums. At the same time, however, there was little evidence of any continuing religious attachments to icons among new converts. Only one or two cases came to my attention in a three-year period, during which time thousands were baptized.

The most challenging adjustment for many Ukrainian, Russian, and Belarussian people contemplating baptism into the Church was in moving from a purely private religious life to participation in public worship. During the Soviet era, a tradition developed among many believers that religion is a purely private matter with God and that devotions need not be, or ought not to be, publicly displayed.

Tatyana heard about the Latter-day Saints in 1991 through a friend who arranged for her to be taught by the missionaries. Though interested, she was not ready to attend church. But then a turning point came, as she explains:

> Speaking truthfully, I did not desire much to visit the Church because I considered that God must be in the heart of each person; and in order to speak with God, it was not necessary to have any kind of special building or public religious service. But on the first Sunday of September 1993, I decided to come to the Church in order that my son, who reads much and is spiritually developing, could find his own way to God.
>
> The first part of the service was interesting, but when we started to sing the hymn "O Savior, Stay This Night with Me" ["Abide with Me; 'Tis Eventide," *Hymns,* no. 165], I felt that my soul was crying out. My soul was flying like a

bird. I understood that it was important for me to come back there again and make a commitment for baptism.

Tatyana's son, Denis, describes this experience in similar fashion: "My mother and I came to visit a meeting of the branch. I was surprised by the Church hymns. I had never heard such beautiful songs like those ones. They had simple words, and they sounded heavenly and beautiful." Soon both Tatyana and Denis were ready for baptism.

Olga is a young university student who had always wanted to find God's love and the love of other people, but she had resisted invitations to attend other churches because she was afraid of public worship. She justified this reticence by saying to herself: "If God loves me, it doesn't matter where I pray to Him. I can do it by myself."

Olga and her mother, Larisa, met Sister Cynthia Robbins and Sister Melinda Richards on the street. These missionaries invited them to church, but instead Larisa and Olga, desiring to be taught the gospel, invited them to their home. It did not take Olga and Larisa long to receive a strong spiritual witness of the restored gospel, and they accepted the invitation to be baptized. Olga and Larisa had not yet attended church and were told that this was an important requirement for baptism.

A short time later, Olga attended the a Latter-day Saint worship service but afterwards was assailed with doubts. Thinking about the experience for several days afterward, she decided against baptism. But because she had lost the missionaries' telephone number and thus could not tell them of her decision, she and her mother attended church the next Sunday so they could speak with the missionaries.

This time at church, however, Olga had a wonderful spiritual experience during the sacrament service and afterward felt the great love of the members toward one another and toward her. She recalls:

> That Sunday changed my life forever. I understood through the Spirit that I had to belong to this church. I saw

such a great faith and kindness on the faces of the people! I felt how their faith was penetrating into my soul. I understood everything without words. I understood that my fear after the first Sunday was a temptation of Satan.

The feeling that I received right after my baptism cannot be described in words. I just can say that it seemed to me that I was flying twenty centimeters above the ground on my way home. I loved everyone; I was so happy. I felt that I was a beloved daughter of my almighty and kind Father. I wanted to hug all the world. I was thankful to God for helping me to find a beautiful church family. I was thankful for being in this church family with my mother.

Eight months later, Olga's father came back to the family after a period of separation, received the gospel and baptism, and was later ordained to the Melchizedek Priesthood. Olga's joy was full: "I cannot find the words in Russian or any other language to describe my feelings and blessings since my baptism. Now I have my entire family in the gospel, and I am eagerly looking forward to going to the temple together with my father and mother."

Aleksandr is a student in post-secondary education. He had not been baptized as an infant and was not taught anything about religion in his home because his father was a member of the Communist Party. His grandmother was, however, a religious believer. After he turned eighteen, Aleksandr began to investigate the teachings of the Catholic, Orthodox, and some other churches. "I did not want to be baptized into any of these churches because I had often heard my grandmother say: 'The main thing is to have God in your own heart.'"

Even during the Gorbachev era and afterward, it still seemed risky to many people to publicly reveal their religious sentiments. Parents especially taught their children to be careful about religious affiliation, for fear that educational opportunities might be denied them. It was safer to simply "keep God in your own heart," as Aleksandr's grandmother had counseled him.

In the summer of 1993, some of Aleksandr's friends at his institute were studying with the missionaries of the LDS Church, and they invited him to attend a Sunday service. That was a turning point for him, as he explains:

> I saw many happy and kind people there who wanted to help me. I could see that my friends had been changed and that they had a new purpose in their lives. After this experience I began to ponder about my life. I understood that I was wasting a lot of my time unproductively. I understood that alcohol and tobacco were taking away my health and energy. Those kind of thoughts helped me to quit bad habits and to do better in my studies.
>
> On the 13th of October I met Elder [Rex] Griffiths, and he began to teach me. I learned about the Book of Mormon and began to read it. Also I learned about prayer, and I began to pray and speak to my Father in Heaven. I felt a great inner power that dwelt in my heart. I began to believe firmly in the existence of our Eternal Father and his son Jesus Christ.
>
> I couldn't feel the power of the Holy Ghost completely before my baptism, but afterward I could feel and use this power much more. I read the scriptures with faith, and my experience is growing with each line that I read. I am not involved in any outside social life, but only in the Church, where I see how people help me and love me. I want to do a lot of work in the Church. I am happy to help my brothers and sisters and others outside the Church in every way I can.
>
> Now I am a member of a big, friendly family in the gospel, and I have found a great joy and happiness. I live by the principles and laws of the gospel, and I have a new purpose, hope, and love. When I read the scriptures, I receive strength to overcome all barriers of life. And the greatest thing is that I receive blessings and faith, and it helps me to fulfill my callings in the Church.

Learning to Serve and Lead

As soon as possible after the Church began holding services in a neighborhood (usually within two or three months), a branch would be organized in which local members assumed all ministering, teaching, and administrative positions, including branch president. Missionaries would serve as advisers and trainers to local officers, teach investigators in Sunday School, and be companions for local brethren in home teaching, but the missionaries held no leadership positions.

Colleen and I, assisted by several senior missionary couples, provided regular, systematic training seminars for priesthood, Relief Society, and other auxiliary officers at the branch level. When member districts were organized, this training was provided by local district leaders after they had been trained by mission personnel.

At first there were no training or curriculum materials translated into local languages. The area office gradually developed curriculum materials in the Russian language. The Ukrainian translation program in Kiev was developing curriculum materials in Ukrainian. The systematic training of leaders was conducted orally, with printed notes of the presentation distributed at the close of each session to all participants.

Although they were new converts without previous experience in seeing the Church in operation, those called to leadership positions had an often amazing ability to immediately grasp the essentials of their calling, as if they had been lifelong Latter-day Saints. I attribute this to some of the spiritual gifts granted through the Holy Ghost, which are described in the forty-sixth section of the Doctrine and Covenants. Some members are given by the Holy Ghost administrative talents, while others are granted wisdom, discernment, and special knowledge beyond any experience they may previously have had (see D&C 46:11–26).

There were numerous instances of the miracle of spiritual leadership granted by the Holy Ghost, but I must confine this account to a few examples. I think of the wisdom of a branch president called to his leadership position after only two months as a member of the Church. He had grasped on his own, through the Spirit, that his most important and effective duty was in personal interviewing and counseling, rather than in other administrative roles, which could be delegated. I sat in on some of these interviews and marveled at his wisdom, discernment, patience, and love. In this way he knew his flock, helped to solve many problems, and strengthened many lives.

Every member received a calling from him. No one sat on the sidelines or fell away. He quickly built a strong, spiritually united, rapidly expanding branch. Today, several years later, he is a successful district president, beloved of the Saints. He had little training before receiving his calling. He was blessed with a spiritual gift of leadership.

When I think of the power of the Spirit to bless the lives of the Saints through service, I cannot forget Vladimir. When I first met him, Vladimir was a tall, painfully shy young man in his twenties. Although worthy, he was terrified when called to be a counselor in his branch's elders quorum presidency.

After several months' experience, Vladimir had grown in confidence, enabling him to accept the call to be the president of the quorum. There was no *Melchizedek Priesthood Leadership Handbook* translated into his language, and he had no experienced high council adviser to assist him. Yet, the marvelous, spiritual gift of leadership with which he was blessed in the succeeding period would make him a worthy model for priesthood leaders everywhere. His personal ministering, organizing, and teaching skills brought the elders and prospective elders of his quorum together in a unity of purpose and action. They excelled as home teachers in blessing the lives of others. Vladimir was later called as a district high councillor to work with all the elders quorum presidents in his district.

At the same time, Vladimir taught seminary for the youth of his branch. He mastered the various teaching techniques that the area and mission Church education coordinators taught to the teachers. After attending one of his classes, I came away electrified, having seen him in action and having observed his influence on the youth. The Spirit was powerful, his teaching skills were those of a veteran, and his knowledge of the Book of Mormon was profound. Could this be the same man as the painfully shy, withdrawn new convert of the previous year? I could scarcely grasp the spiritual transformation that the callings of the Lord had brought into the life of Vladimir.

The miracle of the development of spiritual leadership occurred over and over in Ukraine, Belarus, and Russia. Wherever there was a need for leaders, men and women stepped forward to accept the call and were then transformed by the Lord through the Holy Spirit into instruments in his hand for the salvation of souls. In addition, as explained in chapter ten, a number of local members were called to be district or full-time missionaries, beginning in 1992.

"Where Two or Three Are Gathered in My Name"

Branches were deliberately kept small in size so that everyone could have a calling to serve and so that leaders and members would be able to minister intimately to one another. A conscious effort was also made to build and consolidate the Church in centers of population so that members would also benefit from the advantages of concentrated numbers rather than being geographically isolated from one another.

There were a few members, however, who lived in geographical isolation from their fellow Latter-day Saints. A widow and her son, whom I shall call Valentina and Sasha, were among these isolated saints.

Valentina and her eighteen-year-old son, Sasha, lived in a tiny village near one of the major cities of the Russian North Caucasus. Through friends or relatives in one of the Baltic States, they had heard of The Church of Jesus Christ of Latter-day Saints and had a very strong desire to be taught the restored gospel. At that time Kiev was the closest place to their home where missionaries were serving. Valentina and Sasha lived and worked on a collective farm (*kolkhoz*) in Russia, approximately one thousand miles from Kiev. Without previ-

Convert Natasha Karabeshkina in Kiev with Sister Marilyn Anderson and Elder Mark Anderson.

ously consulting the mission, they withdrew their modest savings to come to Kiev to be taught the gospel, checking into a hotel and determined to stay until they were ready for baptism.

Arrangements were made for them to stay with members of the Church in Kiev so that they would not need to spend their meager financial resources during the two weeks of their visit. They were taught every day by the missionaries, attended church meetings and activities, and spent the remainder of their time reading the Book of Mormon and *Gospel Principles.* Before baptism I interviewed them carefully and explained how hard it might be for them to live true to the gospel in such geographical isolation from members, leaders, and missionaries. They assured me of their strong testimonies and of their commitment to live the gospel, even if they were separated from other members of the Church for their whole lives.

Valentina and Sasha were baptized, and Sasha was ordained a priest in the Aaronic Priesthood. He was also taught how to prepare and administer the sacrament, and he received the assignment to perform this ordinance each

Sabbath day for his mother and himself. He was also taught how to conduct a sacrament meeting. They were given one copy of the Book of Mormon, the Bible, and *Gospel Principles,* as well as various missionary pamphlets and the missionary discussions for investigators and new members. Sasha declared it to be his goal to prepare for the Melchizedek Priesthood and a full-time mission. Valentina declared her goal to be the preparation of her son for his goals and to prepare for the temple herself. Then mother and son, investigators for two weeks and members for only two days, left for home.

Although we kept in touch by mail every few months, I did not see Valentina and Sasha for an entire year. Then Elder Hans B. Ringger of the Seventy, president of the Europe Area of the Church, asked me to accompany him on a trip by van through Ukraine and the Russian North Caucasus. A thousand miles from Kiev, we stopped along the way in the little Russian village where Valentina and Sasha lived. We were guests in their humble cottage. Valentina and her sister (a nonmember) received us with joy. Sasha, unfortunately, was working on a collective farm brigade that day and was, therefore, unable to join us.

Although it was midweek, we enjoyed a sacrament service and Book of Mormon reading session together. After dinner, Valentina asked for a blessing of the priesthood, which we gave to her. On the wall were pictures of Jesus Christ, of the Prophet Joseph Smith, the First Presidency of the Church, and the Freiberg Germany Temple, which they had picked up at the mission office in Kiev. Valentina brought us a jar in which she had faithfully deposited her tithes and those of her son for an entire year.

Valentina bore to us her humble, powerful testimony of Christ, of the Prophet Joseph Smith, and the restoration of the gospel. She declared that after a year her faith in the gospel was firm and unshakable, in spite of a concerted, unending attack on them by the evangelical churches in the village. She showed us anti-Mormon literature, written in Russian and published in America, which had reached even this remote village of southern Russia.

Elder Ringger asked Valentina how she and her son had been able to maintain their faith all alone, without the help of other members of the Church, for an entire year. I will never forget her answer.

"We were not alone. We pray individually and together three times each day. We read the Book of Mormon together every evening. Every Sunday the two of us hold a Sabbath meeting together, where my son administers the sacrament, and we bear our testimonies. As a result, we are never alone. We have the Holy Ghost with us each day to strengthen and comfort, to guide us. We live the gospel fully. Our assurance of our Savior Jesus Christ and his restored gospel through the Prophet Joseph Smith are unshakable." Valentina and Sasha also read *Gospel Principles* together every Sunday and studied the missionary discussions and scriptures.

Nine months after our visit to their home, Valentina and Sasha returned to Kiev, where I interviewed him for the Melchizedek Priesthood and for his full-time mission. In all my years as a bishop, branch president, stake president, and mission president, I have never interviewed a young man who was better prepared. In addition to being worthy and having a strong testimony, Sasha had worked long hours to save many rubles for his mission and had learned the missionary discussions, including a number of scriptures.

As I finished ordaining her son to the Melchizedek Priesthood, Valentina's face was radiant with joy, glowing with the Holy Spirit and with her gratitude to the Lord. I congratulated her on how well she had prepared her son. I told Sasha how pleased the Lord was for the magnificent way in which he had prepared himself. I promised them that they would be interviewed for temple recommends when Sasha returned to be set apart for his mission.

Sasha and Valentina are unforgettable examples to me of the reality of the promise of the Savior, "For where two or three are gathered together in my name, there am I in the midst of them" (Matthew 18:20; see also D&C 6:32).

Learning to Trust and Love Others

As previously emphasized, Soviet society left a legacy of considerable distrust among its former citizens, a people alienated and cut off from the personal lives of one another. This was one of the problems the Church had to grapple with as it began in Ukraine, Belarus, and Russia. The missionaries from America and Europe were greatly loved and admired, but it took time for new members to spiritually bond with one another.

Problems of trust often arose in the initial period just after a member-operated branch was established. At the outset, leaders were new and inexperienced, often converts of only several months themselves. It often took time for them to catch the vision of their callings and to become proficient as leaders. Holding any kind of church calling was a totally new experience for all members, although some were trained teachers and others were already skilled administrators in their professional work. It naturally took time for them to bond together as a branch family and as an organizational team.

In actuality, however, the fact that all branch positions were filled by local members greatly hastened the overcoming of mistrust by new Latter-day Saints. Serving one another, problem solving together, praying and fasting together for divine assistance—all helped to break down walls of mistrust and create a beautiful spiritual bonding. This miraculous process happened over and over in the establishment of numerous branches in Ukraine, Belarus, and Russia.

There were particular problems of mistrust to overcome that grew out of undesirable characteristics of the past Soviet legacy. For example, Ukrainians, Russians, and Belarussians had learned to greatly fear the secret police who had arrested, imprisoned, and executed millions of people, especially religious believers, during the Soviet period. When the son of a prominent KGB officer was baptized into the Church, some members had great difficulty in trusting his motives, especially when he was given a responsible calling in the branch.

This dear brother did not hide his family background and served the members of his branch with patience and gentleness, knowing full well what some others thought of him. In the end his evident faith, devotion, and loving service won over almost all of his earlier detractors.

Some former Communist Party officials and activists were converted to the gospel and became devoted, faithful Latter-day Saints. At first, some other Church members who despised Communists treated them with resentment and distrust. It was hard for some Church members to forget past activities of former Communists and to accept the reality of their conversion. The experience of serving together in the gospel was the best antidote for overcoming lack of acceptance. The stories of the conversion of Saul of Tarsus, Alma the Younger, and the sons of Mosiah were useful models for showing members of the Church how former enemies of Christ can be spiritually transformed by the Lord into his most faithful servants (see Acts 9:1–22; Mosiah 27–28; Alma 36:5–26).

Venyamin was a former Protestant minister who, with his family, had suffered much police persecution during the Soviet era. Venyamin's past experiences had given him a deep contempt and distrust for police officers. He and his family received the restored gospel and the Book of Mormon with great joy. They had faith enough to give up their former paid ministry, in circumstances where few other jobs were available, to come into the kingdom of God.

In their new branch of the Church, however, Venyamin discovered that a former police officer, who had served in the same city where he and his family had been persecuted by the police, was now a Latter-day Saint and was the leader of the branch. Could he love and trust a brother who had previously been associated with an agency that had persecuted his family and his ministry? Could he, as a former pastor, follow a new shepherd who formerly had belonged to the agency that had been the main persecutor of religious believers?

This task of reconciliation would be impossible for the "natural man." Venyamin (the Russian form of the name Benjamin) could overcome this enormous obstacle only by the difficult and wondrous process described by King Benjamin: humbly yielding to the enticings of the Holy Spirit, putting off the natural man, and becoming a saint through the atonement of Christ, the Lord (see Mosiah 3:19). Through the assistance of the Holy Spirit, Venyamin was able to accomplish this difficult task; and the miraculous reconciliation between two former enemies slowly, but steadily, came to pass as they served together to build the kingdom of God.

After one local brother was called to a responsible position, I was visited by several local Church sisters who were troubled because they knew he had been a heavy drinker before his baptism. They offered no evidence that he was still drinking after being baptized, but they found it very difficult to believe that he could actually have made such a remarkable change. The widespread curse of alcohol-abusing husbands who physically abuse wives and children has created an understandably deep prejudice among women against many men in Soviet society.

Further interviews with this brother and his wife, as well as spiritual discernment, made it clear that the suspicions and charges of these sisters were untrue. The spiritual quality and wisdom of his leadership convinced the doubters after a time that his life was in harmony with the Lord, that he was no longer the man they had known before his baptism.

The experience of rampant corruption and abuse of power in the Soviet era made it difficult for a few to trust their local Church leaders. They feared that the branch president might abuse his authority, show partiality, or seek to benefit materially from his position in the Church. These fears sometimes erupted when local Relief Society and priesthood leaders were distributing humanitarian assistance from the international

Sister Evgenia (left) hosts a branch dinner party.

Church to the members. The long experience of "unrighteous dominion" by leaders in society made it difficult for some, at first, to believe that local authorities in the Church would behave differently.

Local leaders in the Church realized the distrust of authority that the long, terrible Soviet experience had produced. They accepted a sacred commitment to show the members that they would exercise "the powers of heaven . . . only upon the principles of righteousness, . . . by persuasion, . . . by gentleness and meekness, and by love unfeigned" (D&C 121:36, 41). While there were one or two unfortunate exceptions, almost all the leaders succeeded in fulfilling this commitment, sincerely trying to exemplify Christ in their personal lives, to be scrupulously honest, and to be impartial and fair, loving, patient, merciful, and kind to those they served. It did not take long for most local Church leaders to gain the full confidence and trust of the Saints through their diligence and faithfulness, and especially through the manifestation of their love.

Missionaries did much to show the members of the Church how to love and support one another. Their efforts were a tremendous factor in the ultimate success that occurred. Over and over the Saints would thank the missionaries in their public testimonies "for teaching us how to love one another."

Every branch had some special Saints that instinctively knew how to love and heal others, to bond everyone together. The following account, written in my wife Colleen's personal journal, describes one of these loving and unifying figures:

Evgenia

Her solid frame always occupies
A seat in the mid-front row at meetings.
If it's ever empty,
One knows she is too sick to attend.
From that spot the hymns are heartily sung.
The melody line booms forth one octave lower than written,
But always accurate.
Though her heart is weak, knees arthritic,
And hearing poor,
Ailments never daunt the spirit of Evgenia.
This grandmother of the Central Branch
Was one of the first to be baptized,
One of the first to be endowed,
And the first to throw a party!
Any dinner invitation is promptly returned.
Birthday celebrations are essential.
She cooks an excellent banquet,
And her tiny, one-room apartment
Is filled with the laden table, people,
And her piano.
After eating, she loves to sit at the table
And clap, tap, and sing the folk songs
Of her native land
That her friend Dina plays so well.
Then she requests I play some favorite hymns.
Evgenia loves people.
She insisted on struggling
Up three flights of stairs
Almost every day for two weeks
To give me healing massages for my aching neck.
She gave me soft silk cloth, jewelry,

And flowers for gifts.
She loaned me her music to play.
She saw that I received huge bags of flour,
Personally delivered by her
In a taxi she couldn't afford.
Her love of soft purples and pinks
Befits her soft, grey hair,
Her soft, big heart.
That's Evgenia . . .
My beloved Ukrainian Mother.

—Colleen C. Biddulph, 8 March 1994

There were members like Sister Evgenia in every branch, who blessed the lives of everyone without partiality. They were angels who helped to lift and heal and forge a people of God, with "hearts knit together in unity and in love one towards another" (Mosiah 18:21). They were true builders of Zion, helping to shape Saints who were "of one heart and one mind" (Moses 7:18).

On a beautiful Easter Sunday we fully realized what had been gradually happening for some time. After individual services in each of the branches in Kiev, all the members came together in a large music hall in the center of the city for a joyous concert to celebrate the resurrection of Christ. Professional singers and instrumentalists, as well as excellent amateur musicians (who were all members of the Church), performed with inspiration to a packed house. A nationally known Ukrainian television anchorwoman, our own beautiful Sister Zina Zhuravleva, and her business executive husband, Boris, narrated the performance, reading appropriate scriptures from the Bible and Book of Mormon on the resurrection of Christ.

While this concert was a great spiritual and artistic event, the most impressive part happened after it had ended. Members did not want to leave, but greeted each other with great joy, tears, and hugs reminiscent of the Church at general conference time in Western countries. That the audience would not immediately and silently leave after the performance was unprecedented in a public concert hall in Kiev. The concert hall operators impatiently turned off the lights and rudely herded everyone outdoors into the square.

This did not deter the large throng of members and investigators of the Church, who continued to stand in a pouring, icy rain outside on the square for a considerable time, embracing one another, visiting, and enjoying being together. Only a few would leave. The rest wanted to be together more than they desired refuge from the deluge. This huge, joyous, loving crowd, standing in the rain, was a very strange sight to onlookers hurrying by on Kreshchatik Street in the center of Ukraine's capital city.

Colleen and I also stood in the rain and shed tears of joy as we watched this sight. We were moved to see the love and spiritual closeness developing among the Saints. Although there were no physical facilities to accommodate them on that beautiful Easter Sunday in a cold rain, we realized that the Latter-day Saints of Kiev had, indeed, become a spiritual community—a people of God.

Chapter 14

"CHARITY
NEVER FAILETH"

*"But charity is the pure love of Christ, and it
endureth forever; and whoso is found possessed of it at the last day, it shall be well with
him."*

—Moroni 7:47

Official Marxism-Leninism taught not only that a new ideal
society was under construction in the USSR, but also that a
"new Soviet person" was being created, which was morally
superior to all previous human beings (V. E. Semenov, *Social-
Psychological Problems . . .*, p. 23). During the last days of the
Soviet system, almost everyone could see that both of these
claims were illusions and that, in fact, the peoples of the USSR
were inmates in a social order of pretended ideals and dark
realities, or in the words of an astute observer, a society of
"broken idols, solemn dreams" (see David K. Shipler, *Russia:
Broken Idols, Solemn Dreams*).

Widespread corruption and abuse of authority engendered
cynicism, distrust, a preoccupation with self-preservation, and
a fear of involving oneself to help others beyond the immediate family or one's closest friends. Helping other acquaintances was both risky and time-consuming, and some "gift"
or favor from the recipient was expected in return for doing
so, usually specified in advance. This tradition remains deeply
ingrained in Ukraine, Belarus, and Russia.

As previously explained, Soviet citizens were taught that
state agencies were to provide all the legitimate needs of

people. Thus the charitable efforts of voluntary groups were not only considered unnecessary but also were forbidden. To claim or admit that the "Socialist State" was not meeting all legitimate social and humanitarian needs of its citizens was considered an "anti-Soviet viewpoint."

For all of these reasons, free, unselfish service (or charity towards others), beyond family members and close friends, was a new experience for many of the converts. Unlike Communist ideology, the gospel of Jesus Christ does create a morally "new person." The visitation of the Holy Ghost fills the heart of a true convert with pure, Christlike love (see Moroni 8:26), which is characterized by a loving concern for the welfare of others (see John 13:34–35; 1 Corinthians 13:4–13; James 1:27; 1 Peter 4:8; 1 Nephi 8:12; Enos 1:9; Alma 36:24). This "mighty change" of heart (Alma 5:14) is a process that takes varying amounts of time for different people.

Sasha's Transformation

I will call him Sasha to protect his personal privacy. He is a man in his early forties who describes himself as having previously been a very hard, cynical man. Sasha identified with a character created by the famous nineteenth-century French realist Honoré de Balzac. The character, Colonel Chaubert, declared: "I have a serious disease. This disease is a contempt for people."

Sasha's cynicism came from his background, which he describes in detail:

> I was born in the north of Russia, in what is now the Komi Republic, in a worker's family in a small town. I worked in the north of the former Soviet Union in the system of enterprises of the Ministry of Internal Affairs (the police). I spent my childhood and youth in a place where many criminals—Belarussian, Ukrainian, Lithuanian nationalists, and Germans—had been deported, as well as soldiers

who had been captured and accused of treason. Cruel and wild morals reigned there.

I learned that a strong man always rules and a weak man always submits. My years of studying in an institute confirmed this statement. Three years of working in a colony of a special regime for dangerous criminals amazed me. I saw and heard unbelievable things. Now it is hard for me to understand how a man could do such things.

I did not wait for help from anybody, and I also did not help anybody, either. I often thought about the question of the meaning of life. What do we live for? I asked everybody about that, but nobody could answer me. People were busy with their own problems.

One evening two young missionaries met Sasha on the street of a city where he still resides. They asked whether he believed in God. He continues:

I was confused. I knew from my experience that when someone comes to you in the darkness and asks for ten kopecks, your answer does not matter much, because there is going to be a fight within a minute or two. Earlier, I had considered religious believers to be mentally sick people, and yet these young men seemed like quite normal people.

I agreed to make an appointment with the missionaries. Oh, I tortured them so much! I asked them many silly, cynical questions, and I even supposed that they were agents of the CIA.

Unfortunately (or perhaps fortunately!), I had lost my job then and had time to read the Book of Mormon and the Bible all day long. The experience of reading these two books of scripture hour after hour, day after day, completely transformed my life. I found the truth. As I met with these wonderful young men, my cynicism gradually but fully dissolved. In our meetings and through my personal reading of the scriptures day after day, I became a new person, with a new outlook on the world.

As I read the Book of Mormon, I realized that there are not inherently good and bad people in the world. All of them have a choice, either to follow the power of good or the power of evil. Life on this earth may be unjust, but there is a future existence—even a new world—where justice and mercy will reign, and where we will be judged with mercy and righteousness by our Savior.

Instead of contempt for people, I have come to see that we need to help them overcome their weaknesses and temptations. The gospel helped me to understand the reason for the actions of people. Now I am sorry for the rich man who spends his life concerned only for his wealth. I am sorry for my neighbor who killed a cat that had scratched his new car by accident. I began to care for wicked people, flatterers, and impudent fellows—not condoning their actions, but feeling concern for their welfare. They are all unhappy people, alienated from God, and I need to help them find him.

Since my baptism and the receiving of the gift of the Holy Ghost, I have committed to our Heavenly Father that I will always try to help lift others throughout the rest of my life. As Alma explained [see Mosiah 18:8–10], when I accepted baptism I promised to be a comfort and a strength to others. And I will.

Sasha is a dedicated servant of the Lord who holds the Melchizedek Priesthood. He is a man who shows great love to others. He now manages a new private company in his city.

Barriers to Charitable Service

While citizens are free in the post-Communist era to organize charitable work, serious barriers to such service remain. In the economic circumstances of Soviet society, and more so in the present crisis, all able-bodied males and females in the family (except students) must work outside the home, often at several jobs at once, for their collective financial survival. They must also travel back and forth from the cities to the countryside to raise food on rented plots of land, because the cost of food is so expensive in urban areas.

The dearth of private automobiles means that almost everyone relies on slower public transportation. Shopping is extremely time-consuming after work each day. There are no supermarkets and shopping centers, and the customer must stand in long, slow lines at each place of purchase. The absence of modern conveniences also makes housework a much more time-consuming activity than in Western countries. The percentage of single-parent families is even higher than in Western countries.

All of these circumstances taken together greatly reduce the opportunities for Latter-day Saints to engage in charitable service. The miracle, however, is that Latter-day Saints are rendering aid to one another and to others in the broader society in many wonderful ways! The following accounts of this are only one or two representative examples of numerous instances of loving service that Latter-day Saints are giving to one another and to others.

Latter-day Saint Sisters of Mercy

Tamara is Relief Society president of her branch. She is a professional counselor who is a full-time caregiver in the first center for autistic children established in her city. A cutoff of public funding has ended her salary, but she cannot bear to leave the children and their parents without services, and so she continues undaunted, hoping that private aid for the center can be found, as her own resources dwindle.

Tamara's counselors in the Relief Society presidency must also work full-time outside their homes. All three are mature enough in age that they no longer have dependent children at home, so they give as much of their free time as possible to serve others.

In addition to overseeing the spiritual teaching, homemaking, and social functions of Relief Society, Tamara and her counsellors have extensive responsibilities for the welfare of fellow Latter-day Saints. Part of their care for the needy involves organizing Relief Society sisters to provide help for those who are sick and afflicted.

The cutoff of public funding has placed public medical care in a severe crisis. There are outstanding surgeons, specialists, and physicians in all the countries of the former Soviet Union, but they are severely handicapped by a critical shortage of medical equipment, supplies, and essential medications. Nurses often go unpaid and, therefore, resign their positions, leaving hospitals critically shorthanded. Declining sanitation and a worsening morale among hospital workers place many patients in an environment of grave personal risk.

As a result of this crisis, home nursing by family members has replaced much of the care that was formerly performed in hospitals by health professionals. Doctors prescribe medications that are scarce or unavailable, and family members rush around desperately trying to find these medications in order to prolong the lives of their loved ones. The burden of home care of the seriously ill on their families is very heavy. Others have no family support at all. In the face of such need, Latter-day Saint women, members of Relief Society, have stepped in to help the ill in their homes, much as they did in pioneer conditions during the nineteenth century.

In the branch where Tamara and her counselors served, there was always at least one member whose illness was sufficiently grave that some degree of help was needed. During one period, there were seven members of the Church who were seriously ill at the same time. One sister was in the last stages of brain cancer, most of the time in a coma, and the hospital had discharged her, leaving her care totally to her husband, who had a grave heart problem, with no other relatives or home nurses to help him. In addition, there were five others totally confined to bed, some of whom were convalescing from major operations, and some of whom were seeking scarce medications. All of these either had no family support or inadequate support.

Somehow, Tamara and her counselors were able to organize sufficient help among the thirty-five to forty Latter-day Saint women in the branch, almost all of whom were employed, to provide continuing care for each of these needy people. This care involved prayers, loving spiritual and emotional support, the preparation of meals, washing of dishes and clothing, and the performance of other housework. It continued day after day and evening after evening for more than a month.

The sister with brain cancer passed away after six weeks of loving care given day and night by her sisters in the Relief Society. Her husband was sustained in his bereavement by members of the branch, both before and after her funeral. All of the others were well enough to care for themselves after four to five weeks. The involvement of these sisters in helping the sick and afflicted was an unforgettable example of Christlike love to the missionaries from the West who witnessed it.

Medication and Miracles

The total absence of pain relievers, the critical lack of antibiotics and other essential medications, and the serious deterioration of hospitals led Latter-day Saints to rely increasingly on two strategies for dealing with illness. The first of these was an LDS Medical Resources Council in Kiev, composed of about twenty medical professionals in various fields who are members of the Church in that city. The second was a much greater reliance on the gift of healing through priesthood blessings.

The Medical Resources Council was organized under the direction of the three district presidents of the Church in Kiev. It was jointly chaired by two Latter-day Saint surgeons who were highly respected in their professions in Kiev. Sister Olga is a well-known abdominal surgeon. The council was originally her idea. Branch president Valery Gontarenko is one of the principal heart and cardiovascular surgeons at the famous Amasov Institute in Kiev, which was probably the top cardiovascular facility in the USSR. Sister Rose Bigney, from the United States, served a mission in Kiev with her husband. She greatly assisted and advised the medical council.

The Medical Resources Council included Latter-day Saint surgeons, physicians, a pediatrician, a radiologist, an anesthesiologist, psychologists, physical therapists, dentists, nurses, a hospital administrator, hospital laboratory chemists, pharmacists, and other health professionals who live in Kiev. The council would seek to provide medical information and locate critically needed scarce medical resources in Kiev. They sought to identify the best medical professionals and facilities for each situation.

On one occasion the Medical Resources Council helped to locate a rare medication needed to preserve the life of a Latter-day Saint patient after he had suffered a massive heart attack. On another occasion the council located a rare medication needed for brain surgery, then secured the top surgeon in Ukraine to perform the surgery.

The co-chair of the LDS Medical Resources Council, President Gontarenko, a noted cardiovascular surgeon, arranged for internationally renowned Dr. Kenneth Doty and his famous heart surgery team from Salt Lake City to lecture at the Amasov Institute and perform extremely difficult heart operations there. Dr. Gontarenko assisted Dr. Doty's team in performing nine extremely serious heart operations in one week, three of which were for fellow Latter-day Saints. This LDS team of surgeons gave priesthood blessings to each of the three Latter-day Saint patients before each operation. The surgeries were perfect, and all nine patients were restored to full health. The Amasov Institute publicly thanked Dr. Doty's team and the LDS Church for all that had been accomplished. Later, Dr. Doty sent a large shipment of medical equipment, supplies, and medication to the institute, all of which were gratefully received.

The majority of members of the Medical Resources Council are women health professionals. They freely donate their service to solve difficult problems for members of the Church and their families.

Before they became Latter-day Saints, a number of the future converts practiced what they call "extra sense" to heal people of various maladies. "Extra sense" is a belief in the stimulation of force fields radiating from the body to promote healing in the absence of medications or professional medical treatment. Although both atheists and religious believers practiced it, "extra sense" was popularly performed as a kind of semi-religious folk ritual by male and female practitioners. Many had great faith in the healing capacities of the ritual practice of "extra sense."

Latter-day Saint converts were taught to put away the practice of "extra sense" and to have faith in the spiritual gift of healing in the gospel of Jesus Christ described in James 5:13–15, which is performed through blessings given by elders of the Church. Ukrainian, Belarussian, and Russian Latter-day Saints seem to have developed an unusual outpouring of the spiritual gift of healing. The dire medical circumstances of their societies have no doubt helped them develop great faith in the Lord's spiritual gift of healing, and many sacred instances of this power have been manifested.

Rebuilding after a Fire

Elder Ray Sheffield and Sister Annette Sheffield taught local Church members principles and practices of welfare assistance as practiced by the Latter-day Saints. Ukrainian, Belarussian, and Russian Church members received aid from the international funds of the Church but gradually learned to rely on local means to solve local problems insofar as possible.

In Odessa a sister had the misfortune of a fire, which seriously damaged and destroyed much of her privately owned apartment. Local priesthood leaders assessed the damage and determined that the quorum of priesthood holders would rebuild and repair her apartment.

They called upon three of their number who are professional builders to manage the project under the direction of a member of the Church who is an architect.

Various brethren and sisters had professional skills as painters, electricians, plumbers, and carpenters. Others had no professional skills but assisted in the unskilled labor required.

They estimated the cost of materials, contributed locally

through fast offerings all that was possible to raise, then applied for funds from Church headquarters in Kiev to pay the remainder. They donated their labor on evenings and Saturdays to finish the project in several months. During that period, the sister and her family were taken in to live with other members of the Church.

A similar catastrophe occurred in Kiev, leaving a family of four without accommodations. Again the branch priesthood holders and sisters undertook the project of rebuilding a burned-out home, following the same procedures as in the previous case.

In one Ukrainian branch, a young man developed permanent blindness. He is a musician who plays the piano and especially the accordion very well. In order that he might be self-sufficient, the members of the priesthood sacrificed to contribute extra fast-offering funds so that a high-quality professional accordion could be purchased for this young man. Now he is launched on a musical career, which he hopes will make him self-sufficient.

In another branch, local fast-offering contributions financed the assistance of a severely handicapped brother. Other branches somehow contributed means for some children—victims of the Chernobyl disaster—to have trips to excellent sanatoriums on the seashore in the summertime.

One of the most ousmost outstanding examples of Latter-day Saint charity towards other occurred (and continues) in the city of Minsk, Belarus. Concerned about the numerous children and elderly people who were suffering the effects of the Chernobyl nuclear disaster in Ukraine, Latter-day Saints from four branches in Minsk, Belarus, organized a charitable association under the laws of the country through which they could assist victims who had been transported to their city. (The Chernobyl disaster affected the eastern provinces of Belarus even more than it did Ukraine. The Belarussian government resettled many people from these stricken areas in Minsk and surrounding territories and also undertook to treat victims in state hospitals situated in the capital city.)

Through their official organization, known as "Sofiya," Church members visited and provided loving emotional support to hospitalized children. During one of my visits to Minsk, I observed Belarussian Latter-day Saints serving meals to a large crowd of elderly people. Latter-day Saints provided and prepared the food in the kitchen of a large public hall. They served the food, washed the dishes, put on entertainment, and lovingly conversed with their elderly, indigent guests. The Church was also able to send humanitarian aid volunteers, both elders and sisters, to participate in this significant, ongoing expression of love, and financial aid has regularly come from Church headquarters to a children's hospital in Minsk.

Somehow, in their own extremity, Latter-day Saints have found means to bless the lives of those among them and around them who endured greater adversities than their own. I have never seen greater generosity, kindness, and Christlike love exhibited than among the Latter-day Saints of Ukraine, Belarus, and Russia.

Chapter 15

PILGRIMAGE

*"I will bring thy seed from the east, and
gather thee from the west; I will say to the
north, Give up; and to the south, Keep not
back: bring my sons from far, and my daughters from the ends of the earth."*

—Isaiah 43:5–6

*"Even them will I bring to my holy moun-
tain, and make them joyful in my house of
prayer."*

—Isaiah 56:7

S now was starting to fall steadily, and an icy winter wind
whipped our faces as we arrived at the old Repin Street office
in Kiev at about 6:40 A.M., 23 November 1992. We had come
to say good-bye to twenty-two Latter-day Saints who were
departing early that morning on a historic journey.

This group of twenty-two souls—men, women, and children—were commencing the first Church-organized journey
from Kiev, Ukraine, to the Freiberg Germany Temple. For the
first time, a group of Ukrainian Latter-day Saints would cross
what had been an impenetrable western frontier of the former
Soviet Union, to undertake what government authorities
called "the Mormon pilgrimage." (The new freedom of religion legislation expressly provided for the right of "foreign pilgrimages to religious shrines.")

I think *pilgrimage* is a fitting word, although it is not
part of the typical Latter-day Saint lexicon for temple-going.

A pilgrimage, according to my dictionary, is a "journey to a sacred place" (often long or difficult) by "religious devotees who seek an exalted spiritual purpose."

The journey to the temple was all of these things to those who participated.

Valery Stavichenko, the first district president in Kiev, would lead the group of travelers, assisted by Aleksander Manzhos, who at that time was president of the Kiev Central Branch. Together we calculated that the travel route across Ukraine, Poland, and eastern Germany would be roughly comparable in distance to the pioneer journey from Nauvoo to the Great Salt Lake, although these modern pioneers would travel in an old rented bus, rather than by covered wagon or handcart. The departure and travel time had been planned carefully in accordance with the temple schedule.

A few Russians, Estonians, and at least one citizen of Ukraine had already individually received temple blessings, most of whom were departing full-time missionaries. These Kiev Saints were, however, the first officially organized "Latter-day Saint Pilgrimage" to the temple from anywhere in the former Soviet Union.

The State Council for Religious Affairs gave its blessing so that exit from the country could be approved and foreign visas obtained. Sister Tanya Moskalyova guided this first group of foreign travelers through an unbelievably bureaucratic labyrinth of exit visas and foreign visas with skill and dogged persistence. Brother Evgeny Zaryugin assisted President Stavichenko in making many other detailed and difficult arrangements. Each Ukrainian traveler also had to receive a personal invitation from the Church in Germany before the German Embassy would issue visas.

At the office we found that all of the travelers had already arrived. Most sat quietly with their baggage and provisions, awaiting the arrival of the bus. Their faces registered a mixture of quiet excitement, patience, and incredulity, as if to wonder whether this sacred journey was actually happening. Almost no one there had ever been outside the borders of the former Soviet Union, and freedom of foreign travel was still a novel experience in this first year of Ukrainian independence.

The Stavichenkos would celebrate in the temple the second anniversary of Valery's baptism in the Dnieper River on 25 November 1990, and a few others had been members of the Church almost as long. Most of the group had been members of the Church for about a year and a half. As I carefully interviewed them individually, it was obvious that they had spiritually prepared themselves well for the temple.

Three months before their departure, I asked Mark Penny, a returned missionary from Canada who was a language teacher living in Kiev, to join me in giving a temple preparation seminar to those who were spiritually preparing to go. This was a challenge because there were no training materials in Russian or Ukrainian, and because the Doctrine and Covenants and Pearl of Great Price had not been translated into these languages. A successful course was, nevertheless, organized, and Mark and I took turns leading the weekly discussions during the three-month period. Family history and salvation for the dead were part of the course, and the relevant forms were ready in Russian translation.

Those preparing for the temple were given an approximate financial cost per person for the journey as soon as the bus expenses were known. For the average person, the travel costs were enormous, approximately equivalent to an annual tithe, but these pilgrims were able to find sufficient funds through great personal sacrifice, combined with some real miracles.

The inconvertibility of Ukrainian currency posed some further serious difficulties. The travelers would be unable to purchase sleeping accommodations, food, or any other commodities during the week-long journey. They would sleep on the bus during the continuous two-day trip to Germany and the equal time in returning. At Freiberg we arranged for them to sleep free of charge for two evenings at the LDS chapel adjacent to the temple. Each family would carry one week's

Kiev district president Aleksander Manzhos (right) greets former missionary Gregory Christiansen in Salt Lake City, November 1994. Brother Manzhos has recently accepted a call to serve as president of the Ukraine Donetsk Mission. He is the first Ukrainian to do so.

food, medical supplies, sleeping bags, and other provisions with them on the bus.

As we arrived at the office, President Stavichenko, President Manzhos, and Sister Moskalyova were busily checking to make sure that each family had the proper passport and visa documents, temple recommends, and assigned provisions for the journey. At 7:00 A.M. everything was found to be in order according to plan, except the bus had not arrived at the agreed time. This seemed strange to me because it was a chartered bus, and everything had been paid in advance. We had emphasized to the bus company the importance of a prompt departure so that the travelers would be able to meet the temple schedule.

After 7:00 A.M. there was nothing further to do, except to sit and wait for the bus. Half of the group sat and talked in one room and the other half in a second room; I moved back and forth between them.

Soon it was 8:00 A.M., and still the bus had not arrived. I suggested to Valery that he call the bus company, which he did. They offered various excuses for the delay, such as "The bus is presently being fueled and checked over."

Presidents Stavichenko and Manzhos were not concerned. "This is a typical delay in our country. On Monday morning things often start slowly." Their broad smiles somewhat allayed my concern. Time passed. Soon it was 9:00 A.M. and then 9:30 A.M., but still no bus. When I again suggested that Valery call, the bus company reported that some last-minute servicing and inspections were in process, which would soon be completed.

Then it was 10:00 A.M., and I observed that still no one in the group was showing visible concern. Ukrainians are used to patiently enduring long delays, long lines, and slow service. My concern was apparently evident as well as amusing to some, for Valery wrote in his personal account of this historic journey that as the group waited for the bus, "the mission president was as excited as a schoolboy."

When the bus finally arrived at about 10:45 A.M. for its 7:00 A.M. appointment, we learned the truth from the two drivers on board. On Monday mornings drivers don't have to show up for work until 10:00 A.M. The bus company had willingly made a 7:00 A.M. appointment with us, knowing in advance that their drivers would keep us waiting almost four hours. Our need for an early departure meant nothing to them.

Provisions and baggage were loaded on board. These appeared quite meager to me for a week-long journey, but I was assured by the leaders that everyone was well prepared. A solemn prayer and blessing on its occupants launched this old bus into a steadily growing blizzard. The historic journey to Germany, a round trip of nearly 3,500 kilometers, had begun.

As they had prayerfully planned the journey, President Stavichenko and President Manzhos were concerned that the lure of tourism and the material commodities they would see in the West might possibly divert the attention of some of the travelers from the holy temple. Only a few of the travelers would be likely to have any foreign currency, and if these privileged few went shopping, it might cause some divisions in the hearts of the people. They, therefore, decided to ask all members of the group to promise in advance (before departure) that they would not go shopping or sightseeing, that they would spend every available moment, beyond the time needed for sleeping or eating, within the temple.

Everyone made that promise to shun sightseeing and shopping in the abundant West, to focus their hearts and minds solely upon the blessings of the house of the Lord. This promise has continued to be an important feature of succeeding temple pilgrimages. Mostly devoid of convertible money, they have come to spiritually purchase the pearl of great price from the Master who invites all: "Come unto me all ye ends of the earth, buy milk and honey, without money and without price" (2 Nephi 26:25; see also Isaiah 55:1).

To help all draw near unto the Lord in preparation for the temple, these wise leaders planned group activities throughout the long bus journey. There were times for singing hymns together, times for public prayer, times for the bearing of testimonies, and times for public sharing of scriptures and the giving of spiritual counsel. During private time, members of the group were encouraged to read the scriptures, write in their personal journals, and meditate, pray, or think about subjects in harmony with the gospel. In conversation and other relations, members of the group were encouraged to exhibit kindness, patience, understanding, and a noncritical attitude, so as to avoid offending the Spirit of the Lord.

It took the party ten hours to get through the border crossing between Ukraine and Poland. The crossing from Poland to Germany went much more rapidly and smoothly. After traveling continuously for two days and one night, a little after midnight on the second night the bus arrived in the city of Freiberg.

In Freiberg, at first they were totally lost. After searching for the temple in the darkness and a low-lying fog, suddenly they saw a glorious sight. Ahead in the pitch blackness they saw the lighted spire of the temple above the low fog, as if it were suspended in the sky above them. Spontaneously they cried out, thanking and praising the Lord. It seemed to some

185

that the Lord was lowering his glorious holy house from heaven to earth before them as they drove closer.

Next door to the temple they entered the first Latter-day Saint chapel that any of them had ever seen—what Ukrainians and Russians reverently call "a house of prayer," where they were to eat and sleep. They were greeted with great love by German Latter-day Saint hosts who had waited long into the night for their arrival. Then they were invited to sleep on cots set up for them.

Early on the following morning, 25 November 1992, this first group of spiritual pilgrims entered into the Freiberg temple. A "wonderful feeling of heaven" and of the "presence of the Savior" were some of the ways they described their impressions upon entering the temple. With awe, they described the kindly German temple workers, dressed all in white, as angels.

The adults were endowed, and couples were sealed for eternity. Then those who had brought children with them were sealed as eternal families. Each adult then performed two endowment sessions for the dead on the twenty-fifth and three on the twenty-sixth, in addition to sealing ordinances. Older children and some adults also performed baptisms for the dead.

Gradually, through two, full, wonderful days in the house of the Lord, their comprehension of his glorious promises grew significantly. Sacred spiritual experiences were enjoyed by some, and all were edified in various ways. Many identified with a scripture I had shown them during the temple preparation seminar, contained in the seventh chapter of the Revelation of St. John:

> And one of the elders answered, saying unto me, What are these which are arrayed in white robes? and whence came they?
>
> And I said unto him, Sir, thou knowest. And he said to me, These are they which came out of great tribulation, and

Kiev Latter-day Saints at the Freiberg Germany Temple, fall 1993.

have washed their robes, and made them white in the blood
of the Lamb.

Therefore are they before the throne of God, and serve
him day and night in his temple: and he that sitteth on the
throne shall dwell among them.

They shall hunger no more, neither thirst any more. . . .

For the Lamb which is in the midst of the throne shall
feed them, and shall lead them unto living fountains of
waters: and God shall wipe away all tears from their eyes.
(Revelation 7:13–17).

One of the leaders described his experience in two sen-
tences: "Until we experience and understand the temple, we
are but schoolchildren in the gospel of Jesus Christ. The
temple is the higher spiritual university of the gospel and
Church of Jesus Christ." In similar terms, another participant
declared that the temple had greatly deepened her understanding of Christ and the Atonement.

Each day they returned from the temple to the nearby
chapel to find that the German Saints had prepared food and
gifts for them. Each also received German Deutschmarks, but
everyone agreed that all currency donated should go into a
fund to help support the travel expenses of future Ukrainian
pilgrims to the temple, instead of into their own pockets.
Although but few Germans and Ukrainians could communicate with words, the outpouring of love and gratitude dis-

played by both peoples united all into beautiful, permanent friendships.

After the temple work of the second day was completed, the Ukrainian pilgrims boarded their bus to return to Kiev, traveling through two nights and two days to reach home. Again they sang hymns, prayed, and read scriptures together. Again they bore testimonies to one another of the temple. The return journey was one of rejoicing in the blessings and promises of the Lord.

The beautiful testimonies of these Saints returning from the temple had a very positive influence upon the Church in Kiev. The tremendous spiritual experience that this first group of pilgrims had in Freiberg kindled among other Latter-day Saints a strong desire for temple blessings, inspiring them to make the incredible sacrifices necessary to achieve that goal. This experience also generated a serious commitment to family history and ordinances for the dead among Kiev Latter-day Saints.

The spiritual experiences that this first group enjoyed in the temple were also evident to members of their families at home who were not yet Latter-day Saints. The wife and daughter of President Manzhos were so touched by the spiritual growth they saw in him after the temple trip that they decided to study the gospel and asked him to baptize them. Similarly, the wife and two daughters of Valery Plaksin also accepted baptism after his return from this first temple pilgrimage.

During 1993 and 1994, the number of pilgrimages from Kiev to Freiberg dramatically increased. By mid-1994, more than two hundred Latter-day Saints in Kiev had received their temple blessings, and about 25 percent of these had attended the temple more than once. The first pilgrimages from Odessa, Donetsk, and Kharkov, Ukraine, and Minsk, Belarus, also occurred in the autumn of 1994.

Elder Ray Sheffield and Elder Preston Porath, with the

help of their wives, taught the temple preparation course for succeeding groups.

Meanwhile, temple pilgrimages from St. Petersburg, Moscow, and other Russian cities, as well as Tallinn, Estonia, and Riga, Latvia, also grew impressively during the same period. Latter-day Saints from Russia, Estonia, Latvia, and Lithuania established a regular schedule of attendance in the Stockholm Sweden Temple. Latter-day Saints from the two missions in Ukraine had established a regular monthly temple trip to Freiberg by 1995, and Belarussian Saints enjoyed their second visit to Freiberg in April of that year.

This rapidly growing temple attendance by the peoples of the former Soviet Union has occurred in spite of the deepening economic crisis in these lands, as well as the long travel distances to these two temples. The cost of one seat on a bus to Freiberg, or on a boat to Stockholm, remains close to the equivalent of an average annual family tithe, and in some cases more than this. Many families of very modest means have borne witness that their sacrifices have been attended by a miraculous opening of "the windows of heaven" to bless them with means sufficient to attend the temple (Malachi 3:10). Some of these families have returned more than once to the temple.

Freiberg temple workers have described the special spirit that Latter-day Saints from Ukraine, Belarus, and Russia bring into the temple. They are touched by the faith and sacrifice exercised to come to the temple, and by the great piety and reverence of these Latter-day Saints from the East. They have witnessed them pray fervently together before entering the temple and reverently touch or embrace the outside masonry of the temple as a final act of loving farewell.

On one of these pilgrimages in 1994, the first group of nine Latter-day Saints with hearing and speaking disabilities traveled to Freiberg from Kiev. They had diligently attended the temple preparation seminar and interviews with priesthood leaders, with the help of dedicated "signers" in the local language. One of their signers accompanied them to Freiberg and was endowed first, before assisting them with temple ordinances. In sign language and body language, with tears rolling down their cheeks, these members, after their return from the temple trip, vividly portrayed the spiritual experience of the temple and their love of the Savior.

The Saints in Freiberg, Dresden, and Leipzig lovingly and patiently hosted and served every temple visit from the Eastern Saints as wonderfully as they had the first pilgrimage from Kiev. Often there were special problems to resolve, such as assisting members with disabilities or those becoming ill during a temple visit.

On one occasion, for example, a sister from Odessa began the process of childbirth during an endowment session. She was removed to a local hospital in time for the birth. Medical authorities had strongly advised her to postpone the long journey to the temple until after the child was born, but she was determined not to miss the first temple trip from Odessa. If her baby had been born during bus travel time, the situation would have been much more difficult and dangerous. In Freiberg, however, she and her baby were well cared for.

Both Freiberg and Stockholm are equipped to offer the temple ordinances in Russian, but in the summer of 1993, Valery and Natasha Getmanenko were invited to go to Salt Lake City to translate these ordinances into the Ukrainian language. In November 1994 the Getmanenkos returned to Salt Lake City with six Church leaders from Kiev to complete the soundtrack for temple ordinances in the Ukrainian language. These leaders were district president Aleksandr Manzhos and his counselors, Vasily Lubarets and Vadim Malishkevich (who succeeded Elder Steven Struk as director of the Ukrainian Translation Office in Kiev), and the following branch presidents: Klimenty Milkovitskii, Leonid Denshchikov, and Sergei Chemizov.

The temple pilgrimage of 23–28 November 1992, from Kiev to Freiberg, was the beginning of a fulfillment of the prophetic blessing of dedication given by Elder Boyd K. Packer of the Quorum of the Twelve on 12 September 1991 in Kiev. Elder Packer's blessing foretold the temple blessings and temple spirit that would be poured out over the land of Ukraine and other lands of the former Soviet Union.

The evening after the first group of travelers to the temple left Kiev for Freiberg (24 November 1992), I wrote the following in my journal:

> In my mind's eye I see that this small company of pioneers is only the beginning. I see thousands who shall cross this formerly impenetrable frontier to enter into thy house, O Lord, for their blessings. And as thy strong arm led the children of Israel anciently through the Red Sea and the desolate wilderness, these ransomed of Jacob shall also come to Zion with songs of everlasting joy.
>
> They shall return with the promises of becoming kings and queens, priests and priestesses, of the Most High to build Zion in their own land; yea, to build a people of one heart, of one mind, who dwell in righteousness with no poor among them. On a future glorious day they will build thy holy house in their own lands. Tens of thousands, hundreds of thousands, shall come to receive their blessings there.
>
> Tonight I also feel the interest of anxious millions of Slavic souls beyond the veil who have seen thy great light and who yearn for their deliverance from the prison house. They also rejoice on this historic journey of our twenty-two spiritual pioneers and for their entrance tomorrow into the ordinances of thy house.

The pilgrimage of 23–28 November 1992, from Kiev, Ukraine, to Freiberg, Germany, was the beginning of this process of bringing the eastern Slavic peoples to what Isaiah has called the Lord's "holy mountain," where he will make his children of all nations "joyful in my house of prayer" (Isaiah 56:7).

Conclusion

PERESTROIKA
OF THE SOUL

As the end of our mission approached we had final conferences with the missionaries in Kiev, Odessa, Simferopol, and
Minsk. We also held farewell conferences with the Saints and
last meetings with the local leaders in each city.

In this last series of our monthly leadership sessions, we
discussed the establishment of Zion and the glory of the
Savior's Second Coming. We discussed their leadership role in
helping realize Zion.

The October Palace was filled with approximately 1,500
souls at our final conference in Kiev. In Odessa 340 were in
attendance, in Simferopol almost 100, and last of all, 425 met
with us in the conference in Minsk, Belarus. At a dinner in
Kiev, President Leo Merrill and Sister Merrill of the Ukraine
Donetsk Mission told us about the development of the
Church in Donetsk, Kharkov, Dnepropetrovsk, Gorlovka, and
Makayevka, all places that our missionaries opened before the
division of the mission in 1993.

While it was exciting to witness the rapid growth of the
Church, the opportunity to observe the marvelous change
that the gospel of Jesus Christ brings into the lives of individual people is far more inspiring to me. We had witnessed many
"without God in the world" (Alma 41:11) transformed by the
gospel and the Holy Spirit into people with sure hope and
faith in Jesus Christ. We had watched some who were once
totally preoccupied with material self-survival change into

Priesthood leaders from eight cities of Ukraine organize the National Center of the Latter-day Saints Church in Ukraine. Aleksander Manzhos (far right) was chosen president of this national administration; Galina Maklakova (third from right) was public communications director. Spring 1994.

marvelous exemplars of the pure love of Christ to their fellowmen.

We had observed the growth of hesitant yet humble ordinary men and women into wise and inspiring spiritual leaders through service. Others, enslaved by spiritually debilitating habits, had become free and strong, in harmony with their spouses and faithful to their Savior. Over and over, misery and despair have been replaced by joy and peace. These are the true miracles of the gospel of Jesus Christ and the blessings that come through the Comforter.

On Wednesday, 20 July, the Saints in Kiev put on a farewell party for us in the traditional Ukrainian manner. District president Gulko was master of ceremonies. We were greatly touched by the love of the Saints in Kiev and in the other cities of the mission.

On "Pioneer Sunday," 24 July 1994—our last Sabbath before departing for home—Colleen and I were speakers in sacrament service in the Kiev Central Branch, challenging the Saints to be spiritual pioneers throughout their lives. A considerable number of them sought a personal blessing after the meetings. A sweet feeling enveloped us during these numerous ministrations. It was a memorable way to say good-bye to Saints we love.

Afterward, Colleen and I were walking out of the building with Sister Olga, a prominent surgeon in Kiev. "What were you doing before you came to us on your mission?" she asked. I responded that I had been studying Gorbachev's perestroika as a political analyst when the call came.

Olga's beautiful face changed into a grimace of disdain at the mention of Gorbachev's perestroika. (The Russian word *"perestroika"* means "transformation" or "restructuring.")

"Gorbachev could not transform *[pere-stro-eel]* us," she declared, "but you and the missionaries have transformed *[pere-stro-eely]* us forever!"

I corrected her: "No, Olga, the Lord Jesus Christ has transformed *[pere-stro-eel]* you through your faith in his restored gospel."

Olga agreed. "Yes, he has brought a great spiritual perestroika to our souls."

As Olga and I grasped hands in farewell on the street, her large eyes looked deeply into mine as she declared softly: "No matter what happens in the future, we know our Heavenly Father will bless and sustain us. Thank you for bringing us that hope and assurance."

The Fruits of the Gospel

Before our departure we received from the Saints in various cities some special letters that beautifully express the fruits of the gospel in the lives of converts.

Galina wrote from Minsk:

> I want to express my gratitude for the knowledge about our Heavenly Father and His love for us, and about our Savior and His atonement, which are absolutely changing the lives of our people, their view about the world, and those around them. I can see how the gospel changes people, how it brings forth their better qualities, and how it in turn inspires them to serve others. . . . This is one of

the evidences of the truth of The Church of Jesus Christ of Latter-day Saints.

Lyubov wrote from Minsk about the many family problems she and her husband and children had overcome through accepting the gospel, concluding:

> And now it has already been eleven months since we joined The Church of Jesus Christ of Latter-day Saints. I cannot express the joy and peace that now fills my soul. Our lives have changed so much for the better as a family! We feel the support of our brothers and sisters. All of us have callings, and we strive to serve and share the gospel with others. We have come to understand the scriptures. We love the Book of Mormon and know that it is true. We pray to the Lord for His help, and receive from Him great blessings, and the Holy Ghost has become our helper and comforter.
>
> And I, as a mother, cannot fully express the gratitude I feel to the Lord for the missionaries who help to strengthen our family. Our family prepares and prays that we will be worthy and ready to go to the temple, and we have no greater desire.

Vadim, a scholar and linguist, wrote from Kiev:

> In the course of my life before I heard the restored gospel, I managed to collect a sackful of sins. And now I can truly declare: forgiveness exists! "Come now, and let us reason together, saith the Lord: though your sins be as scarlet, they shall be as white as snow; though they be red like crimson, they shall be as wool" (Isaiah 1:18).
>
> Let the whole world try to change my mind about the truthfulness of this Isaiah prophecy. I would rather deny the fact of my personal existence. I have experienced the Atonement in my own life. "And oh, what joy, and what marvelous light I did behold; yea, my soul was filled with joy as exceeding as was my pain!" (Alma 36:20).
>
> How can I deny the mercy and grace of our Savior as well as His reality, having received such marvelous blessings from Him?

Statue of St. Vladimir in Kiev, Ukraine.

Taking Our Leave

I was extremely busy during the final forty-eight hours before the arrival of the new mission president, but not too busy to visit two cherished places. St. Vladimir's (Volody- myr's) statue overlooking the city and the Dnieper River was revered because of Elder Boyd K. Packer's dedicatory prayer there. It was wonderful to look down on the city and river and contemplate the fulfillment already of prophecies uttered by a modern apostle of Christ from that peaceful spot.

My other favorite place was a certain park bench in Taras Shevchenko Park by Kiev University, where I had sat alone for several hours on a Sabbath day during an earlier research visit in the 1970s, reading my scriptures and deeply yearning for the freedom to teach the gospel to those sitting by me. I could not know then that fifteen years later I would preside over a mission in Kiev whose first office would be at the edge of that very park and whose present office and mission home are only a couple of blocks away.

For the first year of our mission, I walked past that very park bench every day on my way to the office. Each time I paused, remembered, and thanked the Lord. Truly he grants our deepest worthy desires.

On Monday, 25 July 1994, I sat on that bench one last time and thanked the Lord for the beloved calling that was coming to an end. Paraphrasing Alma, I said to myself: "Oh, if I could have the wish of my heart it would be to serve here simply as a missionary until the Savior comes. But I do sin in my wish and ought to be content with the marvelous things which the Lord has allotted unto me" (see Alma 29:1–8).

He had allotted unto us the ministry of breaking virgin soil, to plow the first furrows, to sow seeds that others would reap, to impart a vision of the future harvest to local stewards who would complete the glorious task. I would ever rejoice in this calling and give thanks for the Lord's marvelous support and answers to our prayers.

On Wednesday, 27 July, we greeted the Lamont family at Borispol International Airport in Kiev. President Neil Lamont would succeed me as mission president. We visited with him the rest of that day and the following morning.

Brother Sergei, our faithful and beloved driver, and his wife, Raisa, insisted that we stay in their newly modernized apartment on our last night. Sergei had carefully modernized and rebuilt every room himself in his spare time during two years of labor while they lived with his parents. It was a veritable "perestroika of his home"!

We entered the immaculate, tastefully furnished apartment to find a large vase of beautiful flowers in every room with written messages of love, new sheets and bedding on a queen-size bed, the refrigerator stocked with food for the evening and morning. We were left alone to enjoy their home. It was an unforgettable gift of love.

The next day, Thursday, 28 July, as Sergei drove us along

the Dnieper to the South Bridge, I looked out to the beautiful spot on the far shore where we had witnessed many hundreds of Latter-day Saint converts enter the waters of baptism. It was almost exactly one thousand years since the whole city of Kiev went down to this ancient river to be baptized into Orthodox Christianity. I thought of the words of Colleen's poem:

> In quiet similitude,
>   figures in white
>   again enter the blue-green waters.
> With right arm to the square,
>   the sacred ordinance is pronounced.
> The commissioned cleansing occurs.
> From a nearby grove
>   a dove coos . . .
> Sweet symbols of the future.

Now we were crossing this Mother of Waters of the Ukraine for the last time. How I have come to love that great river and the choice Ukrainian people it has sustained for millennia! With my eyes I had to drink it all in for the last time. Softly, to the others riding with us in the van, I quoted Mikhail Lermontov's poetic tribute to the Volga but applied it to the Dnieper:

> O Dnieper,
> Kolybel' maya,
> Kto lyubit tebya
> Kak ya.
>
> (O Dnieper,
> Cradle of my Life,
> Who could love thee
> As much as I?)

At Borispol International Airport we said good-bye to those Saints who had come. Even our nonsentimental driver, Sergei, veteran of the Afghanistan War, was in tears.

Brother Vasily used his Red Army officer's commanding voice to talk a "robber baron" customs agent out of relieving me of an extra four hundred dollars for some fabricated infrac-

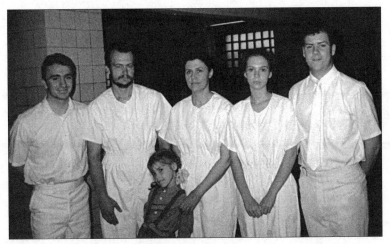

The Dividyk family at their baptism in Minsk.

tion. We sailed through the labyrinth of Ukrainian customs with help from two young sisters in the Church who work at Borispol. They got us through baggage x-raying, then manual examination of bags, ticketing, electronic body searching, and passport control with a minimum of hassle, and on to the new international waiting lounge. (The physical facilities of the dreary, antiquated Borispol Airport were also belatedly undergoing perestroika).

The Austrian Airlines flight to Vienna passed over the Dnieper River and Kiev for one last time. As we looked at familiar places below, the events of three momentous years passed before my mind in a matter of seconds. In a few moments Kiev was behind us, and before we realized it, our plane was making its final approach to Vienna International Airport.

Staring into the late afternoon airport haze, I realized that our world of Ukraine and Belarus and Russia was gone. A great loneliness and desire not to let go of our experience washed over me.

I looked over at Colleen, seated beside me. Before our mission I thought I had known her well after thirty-five years of marriage, but the true depth of her faith and spirit of consecration to the Lord was only revealed to me on our mission together. For three years she had gone through every challenge with perfect trust in the Lord, infinite patience, and a marvelous sense of humor.

I opened the Book of Mormon on my lap and found the expression of my feelings in the testimony of Ammon in the twenty-sixth chapter of Alma: *"Yea, we will rejoice, for our joy is full; yea, we will praise our God forever"* (Alma 26:16; emphasis added).

I realized, too, as the landing gear came down, that three years of living and serving with the beloved peoples of Ukraine, Belarus, and Russia have changed me forever. Their marvelous faith and hope and love have brought about the spiritual perestroika of my soul.

Awake and Arise

Awake and arise, O ye slumbering nations!
The heavens have opened their portals again.
The last and the greatest of all dispensations
Has burst like a dawn o'er the children of men!

The dream of the poet, the crown of the ages,
The time which the prophets of Israel foretold,
That glorious day only dreamed by the sages
Is yours, O ye slumbering nations; behold!

Oh, lift up your voices in song and in story.
Let banners of peace in all lands be unfurled,
For truth, heaven-born, in its beauty and glory
Is marching triumphantly over the world.

—*Hymns,* no. 8

BIBLIOGRAPHY

Act of the USSR Supreme Soviet. "On the Freedom of Conscience and Religious Organizations" (26 September 1990). Published in English translation in *Journal of Church and State* 33, no. 2 (1991): 192–201.

Anderson, John. *Religion, State and Politics in the Soviet Union and Successor States.* New York: Cambridge University Press, 1994.

Batalden, Stephen K., ed. *Seeking God: The Recovery of Religious Identity in Orthodox Russia, Ukraine, and Georgia.* Dekalb, Illinois: Northern Illinois University, 1993.

Biddulph, Howard L. "Religious Liberty and the Ukrainian State: Nationalism versus Equal Protection." *Brigham Young University Law Review,* no. 2 (1995):321–46.

Billington, James H., *Russia Transformed: Breakthrough to Hope.* New York: Free Press, 1992.

Bociurkiw, Bohdan. "The Shaping of Soviet Religious Policy." *Problems of Communism* (May–June 1973):37–51.

Bourdeaux, Michael A. *Gorbachev, Glasnost, and the Gospel.* London: Hodder & Stroughton, 1991.

Browning, Gary L. "Out of Obscurity: The Emergence of The Church of Jesus Christ of Latter-day Saints in 'That Vast Empire' of Russia," *BYU Studies* 33, no. 4 (1993):674–88.

Church News, 1972–1996.

Constitution (Fundamental Law) of the Union of Soviet Socialist Republics, adopted by the Supreme Soviet of the USSR, 7 October 1977. Published in English language edition by Novosti Press in Moscow, 1987.

Dawisha, Karen, and Bruce Parrott. *Russia and the New States of Eurasia.* New York: Cambridge University Press, 1994.

Durham, W. Cole, Jr., Lauren B. Homer, Pieter van Dijk, and John Witte, Jr. "The Future of Religious Liberty in Russia." *Emory International Law Review* 8, no. 1 (Spring 1994):1–46.

Ellis, Jane. *The Russian Orthodox Church—A Contemporary History.* Bloomington, Ind.: Indiana University Press, 1986.

"Four European Nations Dedicated." *Church News,* 12 June 1993, p. 6.

Herlihy, Patricia. "Crisis in Society and Religion in Ukraine." *Religion in Eastern Europe* 14, no. 2 (April 1994):1–13.

Istoriya evangel'skikh khristian-baptistov v SSSR (History of the Evangelical Christian-Baptists in the USSR). Moscow: Vestnik Rossii, 1989.

Keston News Service (serial bulletins of Keston College, England), 1988–1996.

Konstantinov, F. V., ed. *The Fundamentals of Marxist-Leninist Philosophy.* Translated by R. Daglish. Moscow: Novosti Press, 1982.

Lampert, Nicholas. "Patterns of Participation." In *Developments in Soviet Politics,* edited by Stephen White, Alex Pravda, and Zvi Gitelman. Durham, North Carolina: Duke University Press, 1990.

Lane, Christel. *Christian Religion in the Soviet Union.* Albany: State Universities of New York Press, 1978.

Lane, David, ed. *Russia in Transition.* New York: Longman, 1995.

Lapidus, Gail, ed. *The New Russia: Troubled Transformation.* Boulder, Colo.: Westview, 1995.

Lenin, V. I. *Polnoe sobranie sochinenii (Collected Works).* 5th ed., 55 vols. Moscow: 1958–1965. Quotations in this book are taken from the U.S. edition. V. I. Lenin. *Selected Works.* 12 vols. New York: International Publishers, 1935–39.

Matlock, Jack F., Jr. *Autopsy on an Empire: The American Ambassador's Account of the Collapse of the Soviet Union.* New York: Random House, 1995.

McLellan, David. *Marxism and Religion.* London: Oxford Press, 1988.

Mojses, Paul. *Religious Liberty in Eastern Europe and the USSR: Before and After the Great Transformation.* Boulder, Colo.: Westview, 1992.

Osnovy nauchnogo ateizma (Fundamentals of Scientific Atheism). Moscow: Izd. politicheskoi literatury, 1984.

Pazukhin, Yevgeny. "Charting the Russian Religious Renaissance." *Religion, State and Society* 23, no. 1 (1995):57–74.

Petro, Nicolai N. *The Rebirth of Russian Democracy: An Inter-pretation of Political Culture*. Cambridge: Harvard University Press, 1995.

Pospielovsky, D. *A History of Soviet Atheism in Theory and Practice, and the Believer.* 3 vols. New York: St. Martins, 1987–1988.

Powell, David. *Anti-Religious Propaganda in the Soviet Union*. Cambridge, Mass.: M.I.T. Press, 1975.

Ramet, Sabrina P. "Religious Policy in the Era of Gorbachev." In *Religious Policy in the Soviet Union*. Edited by Sabrina P. Ramet. New York: Cambridge University Press, 1993, pp. 31–52.

Religiya, gosudarstvo, i pravo (Religion, State, and Law). Moscow: Izd. politicheskoi literatury, 1978.

Sapiets, M. *True Witness—The Story of the Seventh-Day Adventists in the Soviet Union*. Keston, England: Keston College Press, 1990.

Semenov, V. E. *Sotsial'no-psikhologicheskiye problemy nravstvennogo vospitanniya lichnosti (Social-Psychological Problems of the Moral Education of the Individual)*. Leningrad: Leningradskogo Universiteta, 1984, p. 23.

Shipler, David K. *Russia: Broken Idols, Solemn Dreams*. New York: New York Times Books, 1983.

Smith, Joseph, Jr. *The History of The Church of Jesus Christ of Latter-day Saints*. 2d ed. rev. Edited by B. H. Roberts. 7 vols. Salt Lake City: Deseret Book Co., 1949–1950.

Titarenko, A. I., ed. *Marksistskaya etika (Marxist Ethics)*. Moscow: Izd. politicheskoi literatury, 1976.

———. *Nravstvennyi progress (Moral Progress)*. Moscow: Izd. Moskovskogo universiteta, 1969.

"Two Republics in USSR Are Dedicated." *Church News*, 28 September 1991, p. 3.

Vorontsova, Lyudmila, and Sergei Filatov. "Religiosity and Political Consciousness in Post Soviet Russia." *Religion, State, and Society*, no. 22 (1994).

White, Stephen. *After Gorbachev*. New York: Cambridge University Press, 1993.

Yeltsin, Boris. *The Struggle for Russia*. Translated by Catherine A. Fitzpatrick. New York: Random House, 1995.

INDEX